Make It Real
Strategies for Success
with Informational Texts

Make It Real

Strategies for Success with Informational Texts

LINDA HOYT

HEINEMANN
Portsmouth, NH

Heinemann

A division of Reed Elsevier Inc.

361 Hanover Street

Portsmouth, NH 03801–3912

www.heinemann.com

Offices and agents throughout the world

The author and publisher wish to thank those who have generously given permission to reprint borrowed material:

The cover from *The Rain Forest* by Fred Fusselman. Copyright © 1999 by Shortland Publications, Inc. Reprinted by permission of Rigby.

The cover and excerpts from *Encyclopedia of the Rain Forest* edited by Carol Hosking. Copyright © 2000 by Rigby. Reprinted by permission of Rigby.

Material from *Chasing Tornadoes!* by Michael McGuffee and Kelly Burley. Copyright © 2000 by Rigby. Reprinted by permission of Rigby.

Material from *The Living Rain Forest* is reproduced by permission of the publishers Learning Media Limited, Wellington, New Zealand. Copyright © 2000 by Nic Bishop.

Material from *What's Living At Your Place* is reproduced by permission of the publishers Learning Media Limited, Wellington, New Zealand. Copyright © 2000 by Bruce Chapman.

Images from *National Geographic for Kids* October 2001 and March 2002, *Egypt, Exploring Space, Kids Care for the Earth,* and *Our Journey West* are reprinted by permission of the National Geographic Society. Copyright by the National Geographic Society.

Material from *What is Rain?* by Alan Trussell-Cullen, *Wind and Rain* by Adria Klein, *Tropical Rainforests* by Alison Balance, *Baboons* by Graham Meadows and Claire Vial, and *Eels* by Stanley Swartz are reprinted by permission of Dominie Press, Inc.

Material from *Beaks, Watching Whales, Fly Butterfly, Magnets, Spiders,* and *How Plants Survive* are reprinted by permission of Newbridge Educational Publishing. Copyright by Newbridge Educational Publishing, New York, a Haights Cross Communications Company.

Library of Congress Cataloging-in-Publication Data

Hoyt, Linda.

    Make it real : strategies for success with informational texts / Linda Hoyt.

      p. cm.

    Includes bibliographical references.

    ISBN 0-325-00537-0

    1. Language arts (Elementary).   2. Language arts (Middle school).   3. English language—Composition and exercises—Study and teaching (Elementary).

4. English language—Composition and exercises—Study and teaching (Middle school).   5. Exposition (Rhetoric)—Study and teaching (Elementary).

6. Exposition (Rhetoric)—Study and teaching (Middle school).   I. Title.

LB1576 .H69   2002

372.6—dc21

                                       2002027515

Editor: Lois Bridges

Production: Renée Le Verrier

Cover photos: Mary Metheney and Megan Hoyt

Cover design: Catherine Hawkes/Cat & Mouse

Manufacturing: Louise Richardson

Printed in the United States of America on acid-free paper

06 05 04 03 02 ML 2 3 4 5

Contents

· ·

Acknowledgments

This book has been influenced by so many people, I hardly know where to begin my thanks . . .

Team Heinemann is amazing. Their vision, efficiency, and unflagging support have meant the world to me. Lesa Scott, Leigh Peake, Lois Bridges, Mike Gibbons, Renée Le Verrier, Maura Sullivan, Deb Burns, Karen Clausen, Patty Adams, Abby Heim, and so many others propel ideas into realities. I thank them so much.

The teachers profiled in the Teacher-to-Teacher sections of this book are individuals I have either worked with or met in seminars. Their voices and experiences are powerful windows into the power of our professionalism. I salute their wonderful work and thank them, sincerely, for taking time to share their experiences and knowledge.

My family . . . Steve, my wonderful husband of thirty years, and our children, Brenden, Megan, and Kyle, are my anchors. They bring joy into each day in ways that mean so much. They are the ones who keep me going, offering support and encouragement, taking over my share of the family jobs, and offering love in untold ways so that I could take the time to write. While Steve and the boys offered encouragement and support, Megan played a key role in the completion of this manuscript. She built the art and permissions files, spent countless hours at the copy machine, and worked as an invaluable partner in compiling the pieces that eventually became this book. I am so lucky to have my family beside me.

Recipe for Informational Literacy

Measure 2 heaping cups of curiosity

Add 1 caring teacher

Stir gently with interesting information

Allow to steep in student-generated questions

Blend in time to read and time to write

Sprinkle generously with think alouds, reading strategies, and craft
   lessons for informational writing

Add a dash of hands-on experience

Mix thoroughly with small-group instruction and assessment

Whisk in a rich mix of tools for gaining meaning

Simmer in an atmosphere where information is celebrated all day

Spread over a lifetime of reading and writing

By Linda Hoyt

Make It Real
Strategies for Success
with Informational Texts

Part One
Move Over Fiction

*I*n this Information Age the importance of being able to read
and write informational texts critically and well cannot be
overstated. Informational literacy is central to success, and even survival, in
schooling, the workplace and the community.

Nell Duke

1

Through a New Lens: Informational Text at the Heart of Reading

As I reflect back on the years I have spent in education, I realize, once again, that hindsight is a wonderful thing . . . As a classroom teacher and later as a reading specialist, I fed students a steady diet of fiction and cautiously tiptoed around science and social studies texts. I knew I needed to work with informational text, but I really wasn't sure about how to best support children in nonfiction. I had great confidence with fiction and knew exactly how to scaffold and support readers. In content area reading, I had little personal confidence. I didn't understand how to make the text more attainable or how to scaffold vocabulary and deal with content specific words.

The result was predictable. My students did learn to read . . . *fiction*. But I think back with sadness on the boys, in particular, who would hold books on snakes, insects, and hot rods tightly against their chests as they walked back from our trips to the media center. These were the books of their dreams. The books that allowed them free reign with their intrinsic sense of wonder about the world. I would watch them pore over those books with shining eyes and the power of self-worth shimmering around them.

I think back as well on the upper-elementary and middle-school students as they slumped in their chairs, eyes glazed, while someone across the room read out loud from a textbook. The body language said so much. They clearly were not engaged as readers or as learners. There was little to no reading involved and, I suspect, very little content learned. What happened to the bright-eyed primary students who craved information and felt the power of their own questions?

My journey into informational texts began several years ago as I read powerful research suggesting that 86 percent (Vanezky 1982; Duke 1999; Parkes 2000) of the texts read by adults are informational (newspapers, magazines, directions, recipes, menus, and so on). Lucy Calkins and her coauthors brought about another "ah-ha!" when they wrote *A Teacher's Guide to Standardized Reading Tests* (Calkins, Montgomery, Santman, and

Falk 1998). They remind us that yes, adults do read mostly nonfiction, but we must also be aware that standardized tests across our country are now comprised of anywhere from 50–85 percent informational texts! Furthermore, in January 2002, *Education Week* reported a study comparing American students with students from other countries of the world. The study showed that American nine-year-olds scored first in the world in assessments of literacy but American fourteen-year-olds scored seventh. The study goes on to suggest that educators need to shift the focus to the complex informational texts of the future, providing more time and more classroom instruction in those texts from kindergarten and up.

Informational Texts Across the Curriculum

Determined to shake my own insecurities, I started adding more informational writing to my curriculum. I had students do more writing about the visuals in their texts, about science experiments, about math, and so on. That felt pretty comfortable. Next, I started infusing informational texts into guided reading. During language arts time, we were now reading about butterflies, spiders, and hot air balloons. The students loved it and I felt so successful. Vulnerable students such as English Language Learners and learning disabled students (Batzle 2002) especially bloomed with this shift. The informational texts were without cultural barriers and I could provide experiences that related directly to the reading. This made it easier to support vocabulary in a meaningful way and to help students connect their world knowledge to reading and writing. My third step was to wonder how I might begin teaching reading strategies during science and social studies investigations. Could I use these texts to teach reading strategies? Could I have two goals in science, one for the content and one for a reading strategy? The answer, of course, was yes!

We also realized how important it was to abandon the term *nonfiction*. All that tells us is that this *isn't* fiction. The terms "informational texts" or "info texts" give us a much clearer picture of what these texts *are* and remind us clearly that we are reading to learn information, reading to pursue our own questions and interests.

The rewards from these shifts were exciting. The students were enthused and fully engaged in learning. They started bringing artifacts from home related to the books we were reading on insects, birds, snakes, and so on. Their natural interest and curiosity about the world bloomed. One first grader gleefully stated, "We are learning about the world AND learning how to read!"

As I journeyed with my students into the world of informational texts, we carefully listed the strategies that best helped us to learn from the texts and to continue our growth as readers.

TIPS for Reading Informational Texts

- Think about what you already know on this topic
- Preview the text before reading

    Look at illustrations, charts, headings, bolded words

- Think of questions about the topic
- Predict topic words you think will appear in this passage
- As you read, take it slowly
- Consciously think about what you are learning and what might be important
- Use the pictures
- Look at charts, maps, illustrations
- When you find challenging words use what you know about reading

    Use the pictures, think about what makes sense, use the context, look at the beginning and ending sounds, chunk the word

- Find the BIG ideas
- Make connections
- Notice the author's style. Are descriptions clear enough to help you understand?
- Stop often and THINK

    What have I learned?

    Can I visualize this?

    What are my questions now?

- When you don't understand, STOP and reread
- When you are finished, think about what you read.

    What was most important?

    Were there any confusing areas you should reread?

    Are there any parts of the text you should mark as being most important?

- Talk to a partner. Tell each other what you have learned.

My Informational Text Reading Strategies

- Look at Pictures

- Wonder About the Topic

- Pick a Starting Point

- Read to Answer a Question

My next step involved looking at the approaches within my balanced literacy program and asking myself a strategic question, "Are students spending *at least* 50 percent of each of these time blocks with informational text?"

Balanced Literacy Daily Plan

Reading	% Fiction	% Nonfiction	Writing	% Fiction	% Nonfiction
Read Aloud			Modeled Writing		
Shared Book/Text Experiences			Shared Writing/ Interactive Writing		
Guided Reading			Guided Writing		
Literature Circles					
Independent Reading			Independent Writing (Writers Workshop)		

Once again I had to stop and think. I had added a lot of informational text experiences but I needed to go further. It was time to look at each of these dimensions carefully. I needed to again move beyond what was comfortable.

As I continued to question my practices and infuse more and more informational text into each day, I found many benefits. First, the curricular load started feeling lighter. I realized that I was doing a much better job of linking up the curriculum. The science unit topic became the focus of my read aloud, shared book experience, and interactive writing. I didn't organize everything around themes, but the links were there. I was teaching skills and strategies during language arts time, just as before, but I was also hitting on science and social studies goals. During science and social studies, I was teaching content, just as before, but now I was also teaching reading strategies. I saw science and social studies texts with new eyes. They were no longer just vehicles for content, they were now tools for reading instruction as well. We could use these texts for working on word solving strategies, grammar, comprehension, shared reading on the overhead, and so much more.

Best of all, I saw that students' natural curiosities were aroused. They weren't reading because they needed to or reading to earn points in a program. They were reading because of their own personal interests, questions, and curiosity. Margaret Mooney once mentioned how important it is for students to have a "fire in the belly for reading." My students had found the fire and were blooming.

Self-Reflective Questions

- Do fiction and nonfiction stand on equal footing in my classroom?

- When I look at my classroom library, how well is informational text represented? Is the collection at least 50 percent informational? Do I have a wide range of informational texts including restaurant menus, directions, how-to books, magazines, brochures, travel books, biographies, field guides, books on science, and history?

- How balanced is my Big Book collection? Am I demonstrating concepts of print and reading skills in nonfiction as often as fiction?

- Am I remembering to target at least two read alouds every day (one fiction and one informational)?

- Are my minilessons explicitly teaching strategies for success in informational texts?

- During independent reading, am I supporting students in balancing their personal reading?

- Are guided reading selections at least 50 percent informational?

- Am I teaching reading during science and social studies investigations?

- Am I modeling informational writing and demonstrating a wide variety of forms and features such as diagrams and cutaways?

- Are interactive writing sessions connecting to use of the informational text features I have been modeling or to content area studies?

- How could guided writing experiences improve my students' ability to write informational texts?

- How well are my students balancing their writing during Writers Workshop? Are they using a wide variety of informational text forms and features?

Improving Reading Comprehension with Informational Texts

Key Points for Instruction

- Provide *explicit instruction in comprehension strategies* within the contexts of meaningful informational texts as well as fiction. Emphasize demonstrations and think alouds to make processes transparent to students. Use a gradual release of responsibility model to provide modeling, guided practice, and independent practice (Hoyt 2000) to ensure that students apply comprehension strategies in informational texts.

- Rethink schedules to *increase the amount of time students spend actually reading* and writing in a wide range of informational genres. Students must have TIME with text to solidify their understanding of meaning-seeking strategies (Allington 2000). They must also have a clear understanding that the strategies you use in story reading will not necessarily help you in a science text or your computer manual.

- Ensure that the *learning environment is rich in concept development.* Prior knowledge has an enormous impact on comprehension (Keene and Zimmerman 1997). Build oral language around content learning so that reading about the topic is a natural extension of prior knowledge.

- Build in opportunities to *talk about texts.* Discussions about the meanings and structures of different texts enrich understanding and increase transfer to long-term memory (Duthie 1996).

- *Look closely at your learners.* Build instruction on their needs rather than following the dictates of a program or the sequence of chapters within a text. Observation of reading strategies and assessments of comprehension in many different kinds of texts, including informational texts, can be used to strengthen daily instruction (Taberski 2000).

2

Read Alouds
Celebrating Informational Texts

Reading to children is one of the most important ways we can facilitate their development as readers. We know this and often find great personal pleasure in the joys of reading to children.

But what about informational texts? We know that info texts fill our world and comprise the vast majority of reading done in adulthood, in content area classes, and in contemporary standardized tests. Why not read *to* our students from these texts? So, everyday I propose we have at least two read aloud times. One for fiction and one for nonfiction!

Informational texts have language patterns that are vastly different from those of oral speech and most certainly different from fiction. Read alouds bring those language patterns to the learner in a comfortable, nonthreatening way while providing a window into how a proficient reader engages with informational text. Most of all, nonfiction read alouds demonstrate that reading for information is interesting and fun.

Selecting Informational Read Alouds

When selecting informational read alouds I try to represent a wide range of nonfiction texts such as newspapers, magazines, travel logs, brochures, essays, letters to the editor, directions, biographies, topic-specific pieces (books about cats, oceans, and so on), *T.V. Guides*, book reviews, catalogues, textbook entries, informational picture books, menus, and even dictionaries!

I even bolster my listening center by flipping on the tape recorder during my informational read alouds. This way I can make audiotapes of informational books to place in the listening center without having to take a lot of extra time to prepare the tapes.

Teaching Opportunities with Informational Read Alouds

While I would never give up the joy of reading fiction to students, I am enthused about the wide range of opportunities that arise when we add informational read alouds to our daily routine.

DURING INFORMATIONAL READ ALOUDS, I CAN:

- challenge and stretch the listening comprehension of students as they think in terms of information rather than just entertainment
- make connections to science and social studies by building content knowledge
- expose students to real-life issues that are outside of their current experience
- model strategies for dipping in and out of an informational text rather than reading from start to finish
- think aloud to demonstrate how I access information, make connections, and stop occasionally to give myself time to reflect
- show children my personal enthusiasm for informational texts

Clarifying Differences Between Fiction and Info Texts

To help students clarify their understandings about the differences in fiction and informational texts, I post a chart such as the one at the bottom of the page and consistently add new read alouds in the appropriate columns. With each read aloud, I try to heighten learner awareness of the many kinds of texts that are encompassed within fiction and nonfiction alike.

As students become more proficient at identifying the distinguishing features of fiction and informational text, I can challenge them with texts such as *Pagoo*, *The Magic School Bus*, and *Joyful Noise: Poems for Two Voices*. These selections read like fiction, but are they?

Fiction	Kind of Fiction	Informational Text	Kind of Info Text
Polk Street Kids	Chapter book	*The Rain Forest*	Description
Where the Sidewalk Ends	Poetry	*How to Build a Bird Feeder*	How-To/Directions
Cam Jansen	Chapter book	*A Field Guide to Birds*	Field Guide
Follow the Drinking Gourd	Picture book	*Ben Franklin*	Biography

Modeling Strategies During Read Aloud

I truly believe that informational read aloud time is also a perfect time to extend students' abilities to question, to reflect, and to wonder about the world. As a listener, they can focus on thinking and extending without being burdened by the challenges of the text. Informational read alouds help to expand and deepen world knowledge, while empowering students with "good reader" tools they can carry into their own interactions with informational text.

While reading informational texts, I take advantage of the opportunity to demonstrate the reading strategies I believe are essential. I conduct think alouds showing students how I can make inferences from info text, make connections, pick out key ideas, ask questions, take notes, summarize, and so on. As they watch me move from interest in the content to using a strategy to help myself understand or to enhance my learning, students get a more focused picture of how they could handle their own informational reading.

Teach Instructional Routines During Informational Read Alouds

I have found it helpful to use informational read aloud time to teach routines I want students to utilize during the rest of the day (guided reading, literature circles, independent reading, and content area studies.) For example, during guided reading, I often ask readers to pause, consider the reading they have been doing, and develop a retell with a partner. If I were to teach retelling during guided reading, I would use a lot of valuable reading time and limit the number of students I could support during the allotted time. However, if I have used informational read aloud time to model retelling, my guided reading students already know what to do. I can really *streamline* my guided reading time. The same is true for routines in science, social studies, and literature circles.

I Remember!

Read alouds are a great time to reinforce use of the *I Remember!* strategy. To use *I Remember!*, encourage students to listen carefully while you read. They need to be very clear that their goal is to remember information that they find especially interesting or believe to be important. Remind the students to listen and *remember*, then start your read aloud. When I first teach *I Remember!*, I am careful to read a brief passage, stop, reflect, and then share with the students points in the text that I found to be memorable. As they catch on, I challenge them to share *I Remember!* points with their partner each time I stop reading. They soon catch on to the higher level of responsibility that is required of readers in informational text and put full energy into careful listening and reflection. The goal is to support a strategy shift. When students listen to fiction, they get lost in the story without consciously thinking about recall of facts. Informational text places a different set of demands on the reader.

Amy Goodman, a middle school teacher in Anchorage, Alaska, extends this notion of increasing learner responsibility with an adaptation of the *Say Something Strategy* (Short, Harste, and Burke 1988; Hoyt 1999).

She writes:

Say Something

Amy Goodman

I use *Say Something* a lot. The kids really like it and for middle schoolers, it really gets them talking. I teach it first in read aloud time by stopping frequently and having students *Say Something* about the text to a partner. While this could be a retell of content such as in *I Remember!*, it is often a broader reflection that includes opinions and inferences.

Once students become proficient at *Say Something*, I provide opportunities for them to use it as readers. *Say Something* brings them ownership as they choose partners and decide how much they want to read to each other. The goal is for one student to read while the other listens. The listener is then responsible to *Say Something* about the text. Then, they trade roles. The rule is that they have to read a minimum of one sentence to their partner and wait for the other person to *Say Something* based on what they just heard. The students then switch roles to continue with the reading. They learn quickly that if they go sentence by sentence, it is hard to discuss the content. They have a lot more discussion when they read longer sections to one another.

Pointing Out Text Features

Read aloud time is also the perfect time to point out the text features that support us in informational texts. I like to put a poster such as the one following in a visible place and encourage students to watch for various text features as we enjoy the book together.

Poster

Text Feature

Title

Table of contents

Photographs

Drawings

Lists

Descriptions

Directions

Headings

Captions near pictures

Labels on pictures

Different kinds of print (bold/italics)

Drawings that compare things

Diagrams

Cross-section drawings

Glossary

Index

Questions/answers

Charts

Maps

Graphs

Bullets

Information about the author's research

Anything else?

Read alouds with informational texts are prime times to demonstrate how proficient readers interact with nonfiction. While reading we show our students how to generate questions, make connections, develop mental images, then go back and *read it again* to think even more deeply! Informational texts are often best supported by a conscious slowing of the reading process to provide time to digest the learning.

Teaching routines and meaning-seeking strategies in read alouds work. Amy's success with middle schoolers has been replicated in kindergarten through adulthood. Reading to students from informational sources builds world knowledge, supports understanding of informational text features, and enhances student performance.

Involving Parents

Please remember to involve the parents of your students in balancing their read alouds. Informational texts generate wonderful conversations and help parents to enjoy being co-learners with their children.

FIGURE 2.1 The Klosterman family enjoy informational texts together.

Finding the Best in Informational Read Alouds

The following list of Nonfiction Read Alouds was compiled by Jan McCall, Title I Literacy Facilitator in Beaverton, Oregon. Jan is passionate about children's literature. I think you will find her recommendations to be beautiful enticements to try nonfiction read alouds and to frequently revisit these titles so you and your students can explore their beauty from many different perspectives. As you review this list, please notice how Jan has pointed out the key features of each text and offered invitations to consider these books as models for writing. Jan also invites you to consider how these books might be visited over and over again.

On your first reading, you might just enjoy the beautiful pictures and the interesting information. A second reading of the text, perhaps on another day, provides time to notice the author's word choice. A third visit for deeper thinking supports reflections and connections.

These beautiful books will quickly find their way into your students' hearts and into your collection of favorites for teaching key understandings.

Nonfiction Read Alouds

Jan McCall's Sampling

The books mentioned in this bibliography are just a sampling of nonfiction books that work well as read alouds. In addition to the teaching features listed, many of the books can be used to teach voice, word choice, organization, and sentence fluency in nonfiction.

Brenner, Barbara. 1997. *Thinking About Ants*. Illus. Carol Schwartz. New York: Mondo.
Topic: ants
Teaching Features: cross-sections; cutaways; labels; illustration guide; poetic text

Collard, Sneed B., III. 1997. *Animal Dads*. Illus. Steve Jenkins. New York: Houghton Mifflin Co.
Topic: the roles of animal fathers
Teaching Features: simple main text with much information in caption format; cross-section

Ehlert, Lois. 2001. *Waiting for Wings*. New York: Harcourt, Inc.
Topic: the life cycle of a butterfly
Teaching Features: page size increases as the butterfly develops; identification charts; diagrams; labels; poetic text; supplemental information pages

Fanelli, Sara. 1995. *My Map Book*. Singapore: HarperCollins Publishers, Inc.
Topic: a collection of original maps created by a seven-year-old girl
Teaching Features: maps; diagrams; headings; labels; bird's eye view; flow charts; compass rose; timeline

Gibbons, Gail. 2000. *Rabbits, Rabbits & More Rabbits*. USA: Holiday House.
Topic: different kinds of rabbits, their physical characteristics, habitats, behavior and how to care for them
Teaching Features: diagrams; labels; headings; cross-sections; how-to charts; comparison charts; fact boxes; supplemental information
See also: other texts by Gail Gibbons

Jenkins, Martin. 1999. *The Emperor's Egg*. Illus. Jane Chapman. Cambridge, MA: Candlewick Press.

Topic: a father emperor penguin cares for his egg
Teaching Features: introduction; bold print; font size changes; index; italic captions; use of story

Jenkins, Steve. 1998. *Hottest Coldest Highest Deepest*. Boston: Houghton Mifflin Company.
Topic: descriptions of some of the most remarkable places on earth
Teaching Features: bold print; maps; map enlargements; size comparison charts; captions; graphs; supplemental map with key; bibliography

Jenkins, Steve and Robin Page. 2001. *Animals in Flight*. New York: Houghton Mifflin Company.
Topic: animals that fly and how wings work
Teaching Features: captions; italics; size and shape comparisons; diagrams; sequenced diagrams; labels; supplemental information pages; bibliography

Kaner, Etta. 2001. *Animals at Work: How Animals Build, Dig, Fish and Trap*. Illus. Pat Stephens. Tonawanda, NY: Kids Can Press Ltd.
Topic: descriptions of the work of a variety of animals
Teaching Features: table of contents; introduction; headings; diagrams; labels; fact boxes; bullets; cross-sections; flow charts; experiments; index

Kramer, Stephen. 1995. *Caves*. Photographs by Kenrick L. Day. Minneapolis: Carolrhoda Books, Inc.
Topic: caves
Teaching Features: table of contents; headings; subheadings; pronunciation guides; captions; maps; labels; photographs; diagrams; cross-sections; italics; labeled picture with corresponding key; supplemental information page; table; glossary; index

London, Jonathan. 2001. *Gone Again Ptarmigan*. Illus. Jon Van Zyle. Washington, DC: National Geographic Society.
Topic: the life of the willow ptarmigan and other animals in the arctic circle
Teaching Features: small picture boxes with captions; italics; map; poetic text; supplemental information pages

Longfellow, Henry Wadsworth. 2001. *The Midnight Ride of Paul Revere*. Illus. Christopher Bing. Brooklyn, NY: Handprint Books.
Topic: an interpretation of Longfellow's famous poem that creates a portrait of Paul Revere
Teaching Features: recreations of historical documents; maps; bibliography

Martin, Jacqueline Briggs. 1998. *Snowflake Bentley*. Illus. Mary Azarian. Boston: Houghton Mifflin Company.
Topic: the life of Wilson Bentley, a snowflake authority and photographer
Teaching Features: biographical organization; sidebars; use of story; supplemental page with photographs and quotation

Nicolson, Cynthia Pratt. 2001. *Volcano!* Tonawanda, NY: Kids Can Press.

Topic: Volcanoes

Teaching Features: table of contents; headings; captions; diagrams; labels; photographs; fact boxes; cross-sections; experiments; bullets; bold print; maps; table; glossary; index; some newspaper format

O'Brien, Patrick. 2001. *Megatooth*. New York: Henry Holt and Company, LLC.

Topic: the ancient giant shark, megalodon

Teaching Features: size comparisons; diagrams; labels; captions; colored print; timeline; supplemental information page

Parker, Steve. 1999. *It's a Frog's Life: My Story of Life in a Pond*. Pleasantville, NY: Reader's Digest Children's Books.

Topic: frogs and pond ecology

Teaching Features: diagrams; labels; bold print; captions; headings; lists; bullets; map; timelines; fact boxes; table; newspaper clipping; glossary; journal format

See also: It's an Ant's Life: My Story of Life in the Nest. 1999.

Rappaport, Doreen. 2001. *Martin's Big Words: The Life of Martin Luther King, Jr.* Illus. Bryan Collier. New York: Hyperion Books for Children.

Topic: Martin Luther King, Jr.

Teaching Features: biographical organization; direct quotations; different font size and color; list of important dates; links to books and websites

Ryan, Pam Munoz. 1996. *The Flag We Love*. Illus. Ralph Masiello. Watertown, MA: Charlesbridge Publishing.

Topic: the American flag

Teaching Features: fact boxes; poetic text

Scillian, Devin. 2001. *A Is for America: An American Alphabet*. Illus. Pam Carroll. Chelsea, MI: Sleeping Bear Press.

Topic: the United States of America

Teaching Features: alphabetical organization; poetic text; sidebars; maps

Simon, Seymour. 2001. *Animals Nobody Loves*. New York: SeaStar Books.

Topic: dangerous and unsightly animals

Teaching Features: table of contents; headings; colored print; photographs; writing prompt at the end

St. George, Judith. 2000. *So You Want to Be President?* Illus. David Small. New York: Philomel Books.

Topic: interesting facts about past presidents of the United States

Teaching Features: humor; illustration guide; supplemental information pages; bibliography

Wick, Walter. 1997. *A Drop of Water*. New York: Scholastic.

Topic: the properties of water

Teaching Features: photographs; magnifications; photo sequences; headings; experiments; labels; italics; size comparisons; supplemental information pages; quotation

3

Shared Reading
Big Books and Overheads on Deck

I like to think of shared reading as a *shared text* experience. Shared reading was originally considered a primary literacy activity, but I have found it to be a strong support system to students at the upper elementary, middle school, and high school levels as well.

To set the stage, an information Big Book, chart, or a transparency on an overhead is selected to support the teaching point. Shared text experiences provide an opportunity to model language and fluency as in read alouds, but with a higher level of intensity. Because the students can actually see the text, strategies for using picture clues, boldface headings, titles, captions, and other textual features become visible.

Just as we try to be reflective in balancing fiction and nonfiction in our read alouds, the same need and opportunity exists during shared text experiences. Enlarged texts provide access to visual features, making it easier to show how the author used a cutaway drawing or an enlargement to make a key point, or how the author emphasized important words by printing them in bold type. With enlarged texts it is also easier for the students to access important picture clues and activate prior knowledge. Most importantly, because shared experiences with information books feature real places, things, and events, they are often more accessible to our students (Parkes 2000).

Using an Informational Big Book

EXAMPLE:

Let's look at these two pages in this Big Book. The boldface heading says: *The Lifecycle of a Butterfly*. What might we expect these two pages to be about? What are some words we can predict will appear on these two pages about the lifecycle of a butterfly? What good reader strategies might we use as we begin to examine these two pages? Let's read it together.

Using a Transparency
of an Informational Text

EXAMPLE:

I've placed a transparency of a page from our science book on the overhead. Please take a moment to skim the page silently. What do you notice about the visual supports the author has used to assist us with this topic? How might we use these supports to help ourselves as readers? If we were to make a plan for reading this page, where might we start? What part of the page is most likely to help us make connections and apply our prior knowledge? Please think quietly about a plan we might use for reading this page. What would you read first, second, third? OK, let's try it and see how it works.

Some Informational Text Teaching Points

Print knowledge

Directionality

Letter recognition

Letter/sound correspondence

Chunking words

Phonemic awareness

High-frequency words

One-to-one correspondence

Punctuation

Comprehension Strategies

Predicting from title and cover

Noticing interesting words and phrases

Drawing information from pictures

Noticing details in pictures

Selecting a point of entry into the book. Which part should we read first?

Show how to slow down the pace, skim and scan, preview

Re-reading for fluency

Using context clues

Finding topic sentences

Activating prior knowledge

Predicting words that might be in this book

Asking Questions

Skimming/scanning

Re-read to check meaning

Reflecting after reading: What did we learn? What strategies did we use?

Identifying important words and ideas

Point of view

Building Awareness of Informational Text Structures

Titles and headings

Print features such as boldface or italics

Table of contents, index, captions, glossary

Maps

Charts

Diagrams: labels, close-ups, cross-section, comparison

Photographs

Visual arrangement on page

Language of Informational Texts

Content-specific language

Sentence length

Clear descriptions

Present tense verbs

Language matches form: e.g., directions, personal narrative, menu, all about book, and so on

Shared Text: Using a Transparency

In many instances, the best shared text is a transparency of a page placed on the overhead.

Example I:

Both men and women in ancient Egypt wore jewelry and makeup.

CLOTHES

What do you wear when it is very hot? Probably something light and cool. Egypt is a hot country. People **in ancient Egypt** wore light clothes. Men wore a short kilt, a kind of skirt. Women wore robes or simple dresses. Most clothes were white. Only the rich had their clothes dyed in bright colors. Children wore the same styles as their parents.

Many men and women shaved their heads to keep cool. Children shaved their heads except for a sidelock. This was a piece of hair on the side of their head. Both men and women wore wigs to protect their heads in the sun.

Today, few Egyptians shave their heads. They wear clothes much like the clothes you wear. They also wear flowing robes and light, full pants. Many wear hats to keep cool. Their hats work like the wigs that ancient people wore.

LOOKING BACK

Ancient Egyptians wore deodorant on top of their heads! They sometimes placed a cone of perfumed animal fat on top of their wig. When the fat melted from the warmth, it gave off a nice smell.

FIGURE 3.1 A page from "Egypt," *National Geographic for Kids*, October 2001, is used on the overhead.

With a shared text such as this page, I could facilitate a wide range of shared text minilessons. With a primary emphasis on the content of Egypt, I could work on dealing with unknown words, using headings, finding topic sentences, interesting ideas, or any of a wide range of strategies that would support students at this level.

If my emphasis was on visual features, I might direct my shared text lesson to the illustrations and captions as an entry point into the page, showing the students how I use those to gather my thoughts, generate questions, and get ready to read.

If my emphasis was on the author's craft, I could use this page to develop a compare/contrast chart showing what we learned about ancient Egyptians as compared to those of modern Egypt.

The advantage of a shared text is that students can see the text clearly while you demonstrate strategies, and they can participate as a member of a supportive group before they attempt to apply the focus strategies in their independent learning tasks. Shared text opportunities in which students are explicitly showing *how* to move through a text or *how* to extract meaning will have powerful carryover to independent and content area reading.

EXAMPLE II:

Happy Feet.
Sneakers make your feet feel good. They're lighter, softer, and more cushiony than leather-soled shoes. Maybe that's why sneakers are America's most popular shoe.

BY PATRICK JOSEPH

MARCH 2002

Look down at your feet. What are you wearing on them? Odds are the answer is **sneakers**. Sneakers are everywhere. But how much do you know about this popular footwear? How were sneakers invented? What are they made of? And why are they called "sneakers" anyway?

Rooted in Rubber

The story of sneakers started about 500 years ago. That's when European explorers in Central and South America noticed Native Americans playing with an unusual ball. The ball was made from a milky, white liquid that oozed out of the *cahuchu* (ka OO choo) tree. The liquid, known today as **latex** (LAY tex), hardened as it dried.

Native Americans had practical uses for latex too. They spread the sticky liquid on their feet. Once it dried, it formed a very thin "shoe" that protected their feet from water. They also made waterproof bottles with latex.

When explorers brought latex samples back to Europe in the early 1700s, scientists started searching for their own ways to use it. In 1770, an English chemist named Joseph Priestley discovered that the gummy stuff could rub out pencil marks. People dubbed it "rubber," and the name stuck.

The Right Stuff

By the early 1800s, manufacturers in the United States and Europe had found many uses for rubber. They used the stretchy, waterproof stuff for raincoats, hoses, elastic bands, and more. But rubber wasn't very good for making most things. It got too brittle in the cold and too sticky in the heat.

That changed in 1839. An inventor named Charles Goodyear mixed rubber and a smelly yellow chemical called sulfur. Then he accidentally spilled the mixture onto a hot stove. The resulting glop stayed firm and stretchy whatever the temperature. It was called **vulcanized** (VUL can ized) **rubber**, named after Vulcan, the Roman god of fire.

FIGURE 3.2 This page is from "Happy Feet, Rooted in Rubber," *National Geographic for Kids*, March 2002.

This page, like the earlier example, could be used for a wide range of shared text lessons. If my goal is to heighten awareness of headings, I cover the text box under the heading "Rooted in Rubber" with sticky notes. The students could then use the heading to predict the content they suspect they will be reading. Their predictions could also include words they expect to encounter.

Guess the heading. The process could be switched for another segment of the text by covering the heading and then letting the students read the passage. They could then "think of a good heading for this section." This interaction closely parallels standardized testing formats in which students are asked to think of a good name for a story.

Engaging Students in Presenting Shared Text Minilessons

Shared text experiences are really about modeling and having a skilled leader provide apprentices with helpful strategies for interacting with text. The two vignettes that follow are exciting models of teachers who empower students to do the modeling using shared texts that include the overhead, charts, and even sharing the same piece of reading material in partners.

Barry Hoonan, Washington Educator

Barry Hoonan, upper elementary teacher on Bainbridge Island, Washington, believes strongly in the power of student-led minilessons and think alouds. As he is doing his cross-curricular minilessons and think alouds, he watches for students who have deeper levels of understanding and can apply the target strategies. Then, he asks those students to present minilessons and think alouds as guests in various guided reading groups or before a whole class experience in science or social studies. He also watches for students who intuitively are applying important strategies that have not yet been presented to the class or a guided reading group. These intuitive strategy users can be invited to present their strategies in the form of a minilesson or think aloud even if it is the first time the group has been introduced to that particular strategy. Barry reminds us of the power of peer coaching and the natural intensity that occurs when we give students the opportunity to teach each other. Overhead transparencies, charts, and Big Books are used for student-led experiences.

Melissa Miller and Doreen Esposito, Manhattan New School, New York City

On a recent visit to Manhattan New School in District 2, New York City, I had the privilege of watching Melissa Miller, grade 2 teacher, and Doreen Esposito, grade 5 teacher, carry "Buddy Reading" to new heights by integrating a think aloud into the interaction between cross-age partners who were sharing texts.

In their own classrooms, students read and discussed articles on the repairs made in space recently to the Hubble satellite. Each group used the *Time for Kids* news magazines appropriate to their grade level to build background and ensure that each student had a copy of the text. The second graders read their second-grade issue independently, then shared orally as their teacher recorded the facts they had gleaned from their reading on chart paper. The fifth graders read their fifth-grade article on the same topic, discussed the content, and then prepared a think aloud to share with their second-grade partners. Doreen had been working with the fifth graders all year to provide demonstrations of how to mark up texts to make connections, ask questions, and so on. They were ready now, to share their strategies with their second-grade reading buddies as they read the more complex fifth-grade passage to their young partners.

Reading buddies started with a discussion of the content of their articles. Because both groups had read about the Hubble repairs, the second graders were full participants in the content discussion, entering the conversation with facts, information, and a sense of partnership with their fifth-grade buddies.

Next, the fifth graders introduced their second-grade partners to the more complex fifth-grade passage. They explained that they were going to read it aloud and would be marking the text as they went along to show how they were making connections, asking questions, and creating visual images. (The fifth graders had taken time to plan their think alouds and were ready for their demonstration of marking the text.)

The result was so powerful. All students learned the content, engaged in a meaningful conversation, and the one-to-one strategy demonstration ensured that "teachers" and reading buddies alike really understood the reading strategies.

A Celebration of Information: Big Books for Shared Experiences

The following list of "25 Big Books Too Good to Miss" was developed by Jodi Wilson, Early Childhood Facilitator and Reading Specialist, in Spokane, Washington.

Nonfiction Selections

Jodi Wilson

These nonfiction selections are some favorites. These books provide children with quality models for multiple readings and writing opportunities. Each re-reading elicits new discussion from kids as they tap into sophisticated text features, high-quality photographs, diagrams, and informational text. High kid appeal earned these Big Books their five-star rating.

25 Nonfiction Big Books Too Good to Miss

Title	Author	Publisher	Grade Level
Animal Clues	Steven Moline	Rigby	Primary/Intermediate
As Big As A Whale	Melvin Berger	Newbridge	Primary/Intermediate
Big Book of Maps	—	National Geographic	Primary/Intermediate
Birds of Prey	Marilyn Wooley & Keith Pigdon	Mondo	Primary/Intermediate
Body Maps	Steven Moline	Rigby	Primary/Intermediate
The Book of Animal Facts	Steven Moline	Rigby	Primary/Intermediate
Caterpillar Diary	Steven Moline	Rigby	Primary/Intermediate
Creatures of the Night	Kath Murdoch & Steven Ray	Mondo	Primary/Intermediate
Digging for Dinosaurs	Melvin Berger	Newbridge	Primary/Intermediate
The Gas Giants	Steven Moline	Rigby	Intermediate
Exploring Space	Toni Eugene	National Geographic	Primary
How to Grow a Sunflower	Sylvia Karavis & Gill Matthews	Rigby	Primary
Insects	Robin Bernard	National Geographic	Primary
Life in the Rainforest	Melvin Berger	Newbridge	Primary/Intermediate
Our Whale Watching Trip	Sylvia Karavis & Gill Matthews	Rigby	Primary
Penguins	Marilyn Wooley & Keith Pigdon	Mondo	Primary/Intermediate
The Restless Earth	Melvin Berger	Newbridge	Intermediate
Salmon	Sylvia M. James	Mondo	Primary
Should There Be Zoos?	Tony Stead	Mondo	Primary
Tadpole Diary	Steven Moline	Rigby	Primary/Intermediate
Whales	Joan Short & Bettina Bird	Mondo	Primary/Intermediate
What Did I Eat Today?	Steven Moline	Rigby	Primary
Where Does Breakfast Come From?	David Flint	Rigby	Primary/Intermediate
Who Lives In the Sea?	Sylvia M. James	Mondo	Primary
The World of Ants	Melvin Berger	Newbridge	Primary

4

. . . .

Independent Reading
with Informational Texts
Making It Personal

In our wonderings about informational texts and the importance of providing extensive and intensive experience with a range of informational forms, independent reading of informational texts must be part of our plan. We must ask questions such as: Are my students experiencing a balance of informational texts and fiction in their independent reading? Do I have enough informational texts representing enough different forms of nonfiction to draw the attention of my students and invite reflection? Do the minilessons and teaching conferences I offer during independent reading time address the range of nonfiction forms and strategies students need? Are we spending enough time reading so they can get involved with their topics?

Independent reading time can be filled with instruction as well as intensive learner engagement. When you open with a minilesson (see *Snapshots: Literacy Minilessons Up Close*, Hoyt 2000), follow with a period of independent reading during which you conduct individual reading conferences, and then close with a sharing session. In this scenario, learning is fully supported.

Minilesson

The minilesson sets a standard with a demonstration of how a good reader interacts with informational texts, selects a variety of informational forms, or uses meaning-seeking strategies while reading. I find it helpful to keep a log such as the following:

Teacher Record-Keeping Form

Informational Minilessons Presented Before Independent Reading

Date	Text Feature	Reading Strategy	Text Used for Minilesson

Independent Reading

During reading, all students are actively applying the strategy taught in the minilesson with high levels of accountability. Some of the strategies they will use include:

- affixing sticky notes to their books
- keeping a log in which they record their observations of informational text features
- attaching large sticky notes with informational book reviews to leave for other classmates who read the same book

The teaching conferences are conducted individually. They are brief but focused opportunities for the teacher to gather a running record, listen to a retell, discuss informational strategies the reader is using well, or to teach a strategy the learner is not yet using.

Sharing Session/Reflection

After reading, students can meet with partners to share the texts they read and the strategies they used as readers, then meet as a class to reflect on their learnings during this session. "What did you learn today?" is a question that addresses both content and strategies.

Learning to Sustain Attention for Reading: The "Bedside Stand"

Many teachers report that their students have difficulty sustaining their attention during independent reading. To help learners extend their stamina for reading and broaden the range of the forms they read, I share my bedside stand with them. My bedside stand, perhaps like many of yours, is a special place where I collect the texts I want to read. My stack of reading materials usually includes a novel or two, some magazines, recipes, travel brochures, and books on topics of personal interest. When a friend gives me a book or recommends one, onto the stack it goes.

My bedside stand reflects a wide range of text forms and, most certainly, my interests. It sustains me as a reader in that I never have to worry if I have something to read. I also find that my bedside stand helps me think ahead as a reader. When I have an opportunity to go to the library or book store, I usually plan ahead and pick up multiple books and magazines. That way if I finish one or decide I don't like it, I have something else to choose from.

Students benefit from planning ahead as readers and from consciously exploring topics of personal interest. I see many teachers using old cereal boxes or baskets to create special places for children to keep their familiar favorites. Why not take it a step further?

I provide department store bags or grocery bags with handles and support students in building their own bedside stand. They use the bag to collect magazines, newspapers, books on favorite topics, familiar favorites, and so on. When this bag is tucked up at the side of a reader during independent reading, there are many benefits:

- They don't need to walk anywhere. If they want to change books, they just reach into their bedside stand.

- We can look at the collection weekly to survey the contents for breadth of text forms. Do they have fiction as well as a variety of nonfiction formats? Are there several topics represented? Is it time to rotate familiar favorites? Are there some class read alouds that would be good additions to the collection? Would it be helpful to have some books on tape included?

Keeping Logs to Balance Reading

Christine Duthie, in *True Stories* (1996), explains how she helps primary learners heighten awareness of the balance they are keeping in their reading. Her logs ask students to keep a list of books that were read during independent reading and then color code a circle to show the kind of reading the book represented. Taberski also does this in *On Solid Ground* (2000). This makes it easy for the teacher and student to see at a glance how well the reading is balanced. A quick look at this sheet might broaden choices for the bedside stand, provide a powerful reading conference discussion, or help readers be more mindful of text forms when making their reading selections:

Frog and Toad	O (green for fiction)
The Great Cats	O (blue for nonfiction)
Where the Sidewalk Ends	O (red for poetry)

I like this idea a lot and expanded it just a bit.

KEY:

Green	Fiction
Red	Poetry
Yellow	How-to
Blue	All about _____ books
Purple	Magazines/articles/newspaper
Brown	Picture dictionary

You might experiment with this concept and see what works for your students or consider changing the codes as you attempt to expose your students to additional informational forms.

Independent Reading Log

Reader Name _____

Month _____

Keep track of the reading you do this month. Notice the kinds of informational texts you are selecting as well as how often you read fiction vs nonfiction.

Title	Date	Fiction	Personal narrative/biography	Topic book about science or history	How-to book	Recipes	Magazine	Newspaper	Menu	Field guide	Diary	Biography	Autobiography	Pamphlet/brochure	Picture dictionary	Guide books	Other

Reflecting on Personal Reading
with Informational Texts

Monthly Reflections

Reader Name _____   Month _____

Week 1   This week I have been successful at: _____

              Strategies I used a lot this week: _____

              Next week I plan to work on: _____

Week 2   This week I have been successful at: _____

              Strategies I used a lot this week: _____

              Next week I plan to work on: _____

Week 3   This week I have been successful at: _____

              Strategies I used a lot this week: _____

              Next week I plan to work on: _____

Week 4   This week I have been successful at: _____

              Strategies I used a lot this week: _____

              Next week I plan to work on: _____

Reflecting on Informational Texts: Independent Reading

Book Reviewed: _____ Topic: _____ Reviewer: _____

What did you think of this book? _____

_____

_____

Would you recommend it to someone else? _____

What rating would you give it?   ★ ★ ★ ★ ★
   (five stars is the highest rating)

What was the best part? _____

_____

   Why? _____

_____

_____

What did you learn about the craft of writing nonfiction? _____

_____

_____

How might you use this learning in your own writing? _____

_____

_____

The Vital Importance of Independent Reading

The findings of the National Reading Panel (NRP Report 2001) have been widely touted as suggesting we should not have students read independently. This is simply not true.

The report itself explains that hundreds of correlational studies suggest that the best readers read the most and it appears that independent reading may better children's fluency, vocabulary, and comprehension (NRP Report 2001).

Joanne Yatvin, a member of the panel, reports that the panel found that having students read silently, without guidance or feedback, does not appear to boost reading achievement, but the amount of data was so small that the Panel decided not to make a determination of ineffectiveness on this limited basis. In today's classrooms, independent reading is not likely to occur "without guidance or feedback." Contemporary teachers understand that independent reading time when matched with a minilesson, conferences, learner responsibility, and feedback are a winning combination.

It is not just intuition that leads us to understand the importance of independent reading. One of the strongest research-based recommendations coming from the *Report on Becoming a Nation of Readers* (Anderson 1992) was to increase independent reading. Research reviews conducted by Allington (2001), Routman (2000), Krashen (1993), and the *NAEP Reading Report Card for the Nation* (U.S. Department of Education 1999) all call for more reading time.

Critics of the *National Reading Panel Report*, including panel members who filed the *Minority Report*, reflect a growing concern that the importance of independent reading cannot be measured by experimental studies alone. Experimental studies require a control group that is denied the intervention being researched. Would it not be a violation of human rights to deny groups of children the right to read independently in materials of their choosing just to gather research to prove it works?

We must communicate the value of independent reading to parents, administrators, and the children themselves. We need to educate those who see research in the narrowest of scientific terms and those who are too easily swayed by powerful statements . . . We have research behind us.

Part Two

Learning to Read AND Reading to Learn

*P*roficient readers are strategic. They monitor their comprehension during reading. They notice when they do or do not
understand. They can identify confusing ideas and words, then implement
strategies to help themselves deal with the problem. Proficient readers also
shift their reading style and speed to meet their purpose. Most of all proficient
readers have a rich collection of strategies to draw from as they interact with
the varying texts of our world.

Linda Hoyt

5

Yes They Can! Emergent Readers and Informational Texts

We have all heard the old adage that first you learn to read and then you read to learn. But I must ask, Why wait? As stated so often throughout this book, children are fascinated by the real world. Why not learn to read *while* learning about the world! Knowledge brings us power and the more ways we have of gaining information, the more empowered we become.

Young children can interact successfully with informational texts and there is much evidence that they benefit from doing so (Casswell and Duke 1998; Duthie 1996). The proposal that young children just learn to read while older students read to learn deprives learners at both ends of the spectrum (Guillaume 1998). Young children are fascinated by the real world and delight in learning about it while upper-grade students need to continue to refine their skills as readers of information sources.

FIGURE 5.1 Within the book introduction we talk about the table of contents and what its purpose is. Photo by Kathy Baird.

FIGURE 5.2 Gaye using the pictures in the index to help during his first reading. Photo by Kathy Baird.

Using Content-Specific Language

One of our main responsibilities in the primary grades is to support expansion of oral language proficiency. We know the importance of well-rounded language structures and rich vocabulary. It is critical to remember, however, students who complete high school will have spent the greatest majority of their learning time in content area classes. We need to build the language of informational communication right from the start. Children need to talk about real things, describing and elaborating on key understandings. They need to use the specific language features of information sharing and to see how these language features appear in written texts as well. When young children describe the petals of a flower or the fragile wings of a bee, or show cause and effect relationships by planting seeds and watching them grow, they are actually sowing the seeds of lifelong language use as well.

Reading Development Is Genre Specific

The research of Nell Duke, Michigan State University (1999), suggests that we understand that reading development is genre specific. Reading fiction will not necessarily help you be better at reading a cookbook, directions, or a computer manual. To become successful readers and writers of informational texts, children must see, hear, and write informational texts from the onset of literacy development. They must experience the widest possible range of forms over and over again to ensure that the differences in the forms are clear and that a range of strategies for reading and writing those forms is well established. For example, to understand how texts that give directions work, they can't read just one!

I cannot help but wonder if the challenges commonly seen by upper-elementary and middle-school teachers as their students encounter content area reading would be minimized if learners had a rich background with informational texts from the onset of reading.

The following are key points for engaging our youngest students with informational texts to stimulate learning, pique interest, and lay a strong foundation for the reading strategies that will empower them through life.

Build Prior Knowledge

Take time to talk about what children already know about a topic and any related experiences they may have had. I remember once engaging a group of first graders with a book entitled *Picnic*. A little girl kept raising her hand and trying to tell us about going on a picnic with her family. I also recall asking that child to save her story as it was time for reading. Looking back on that moment, I realize what a mistake I had made. That child's real-life picnic and the background it brought provided vital connections to the learning, enabled her to read critically, and most certainly provided motivation to read. My comment suggested to her that thinking was not part of reading . . . I am so glad that I will never make that mistake again! Now I realize that connections to life experiences and to prior knowledge are of critical importance.

Provide Hands-on Experiences Before Reading

Real experiences build a knowledge base on the topic. If you are about to read a poem on turtles, perhaps you could bring in a real turtle. A guided reading selection on bubbles could be introduced by blowing real bubbles and talking about them. (*What do you notice? How are they made? What is inside?*) An article on skateboarding might be supported with a *before*-reading demonstration by a skateboard enthusiast.

FIGURE 5.3 While Eric blows bubbles he is preparing language, vocabulary, and questions that will help him read a passage on bubbles more effectively.

Before-reading experiences, with real things, activate both hemispheres of the brain and create memorable moments that can be later recalled and utilized during reading (Hoyt 1992). The goal is to build concepts and the language to label the concepts. We have all seen the tepid result of posting vocabulary words on the blackboard and telling students to watch for them in the text. If vocabulary is actively built in concert with language and concepts, there is a rich network of connections related to a topic. Relationships between ideas become more memorable and thus, much more readable as well.

When students have a real experience, then write and read, they might use a chart such as the following:

BUBBLES

Look Like	Where We Find Bubbles	What We Know About Bubbles

When we blew bubbles . . .
You make bubble mix with . . .
The biggest bubble was . . .

The joys of early childhood can be easily brought together with exploration of the world. Linking real experiences with print makes sense. It is fun. Children learn everything they need to know about the world of print while expanding what they know about the world!

Incorporating Illustrations

As you provide these important experiences and conversations to prepare for reading or writing, it can also be helpful to engage young children in drawing about the topic. As you prepare to read about butterflies, for example, students could talk, draw what they already know, label their illustrations and/or write. By taking time to elicit content knowledge before reading, you can assess the level of their prior knowledge, identify misconceptions, and determine their ability to use language specific to discussing butterflies. With this foundation, a read aloud, shared book experience, or guided reading lesson starts on strong footing and the illustration becomes a collection tool. As the reading progresses, they can add information and detail to their drawings and end up with a summary of their learning.

Other Supports

Further prereading supports might include listing words related to the topic on a chart, jotting their observations in the form of a language experience story, or an interactive writing piece. This written confirmation of information through art and written language scaffolds both understanding and print knowledge to prepare the child for reading on the topic.

Read Nonfiction Selections in a Wide Range of Forms

(Please see Chapter 2 on Read Alouds.) Reading nonfiction builds a sense of importance around informational texts, loads children's heads with the cadences and structures of informational language, and, again, builds world knowledge. It is also helpful to demonstrate the shifts you are making in reading strategies when you read for information. For example, you might show the students a cookbook and explain that your purpose is to look up a recipe for chocolate chip cookies. You could then do a think aloud about finding the recipe and tell how you might not start on page 1. In a cookbook, you usually use the table of contents or the index and go straight to the page you need. This is really important as students so often watch us read fiction from start to finish. With nonfiction, children need to understand that we have a purpose for reading and then plan our reading to match our purpose. If I need the cookie recipe, should I start on page 1 or turn to the index to find it quickly? If I am wondering about how a whale breathes, would I read the entire book or turn quickly to that particular section in the book on whales?

Immerse Young Children in Informational Texts

Stand back and look around your room. Does informational text make up about 50 percent of the print on the walls? Did the students make their own alphabet chart using environmental print sources such as Mc-Donald's bags, Coke cans, and other realia? As you look at your charts and poem boards, do you see lots of informational texts? In guided reading, are your emergent students having extensive opportunities to read about the real world? Are the forms you are providing exploring the full range of info forms such as picture books, magazines, directions, brochures, recipes, descriptions, and so on? When you plan a unit of study are you gathering resources at a range of reading and interest levels? If you have a central book room, you might also want to check your collection at each level for balance of fiction to nonfiction and for the range of informational forms represented.

Select Resources with High-Quality Photographs and Text

The resources currently available from publishers of guided reading resources are making it easier than ever to engage emergent readers with informational texts. The newest informational books have all of the features we need to support concepts of print, phonics understandings, phonemic awareness, and comprehension. In reviewing informational resources for emergent readers, I look for the following:

- High-quality photographs

- Text that closely matches the content of the picture

- Natural language patterns

- Careful placement of punctuation (not at the end of every line)

- Common conventions for informational text such as table of contents, labels on pictures, captions, headings, titles, an index or glossary

- Content links to my science and social studies curriculum

- Content that is interesting to learners at this developmental level

The wonderful resources we currently have available to our most emergent readers make informational reading developmentally appropriate and are very supportive of fledgling reading strategies. *National Geographic* has even come out with a new wordless collection of information books called *Steps to Windows on Literacy*, 2002, which is a terrific support to young children at all phases of development.

Concepts of Print Checklist: Surveying Concepts in Informational Text

Reader _____ Date _____

Book _____ Topic _____

While previewing the text, the reader:

☐ Holds the book correctly

☐ Knows how to turn pages in correct order

☐ Attends closely to photographs and illustrations

☐ Asks questions or makes comments while surveying visuals

☐ Shares connections to experiences, other books on the topic, or other sources of information on this topic

While reading the text, the reader:

☐ Tracks the print from left to right

☐ Uses picture clues to determine meaning or to predict

☐ Recognizes when the reading doesn't make sense

☐ Backtracks to re-read for meaning or fluency

☐ Uses beginning and ending sounds

☐ Chunks words

☐ Uses context clues. Wonders what would make sense here

☐ Wonders about the topic while reading

Support Systems for Emergent Readers

As emergent readers interact with informational texts, the following support systems are some that I have found to be helpful and fun!

Personal Literacy Frames

Personal literacy frames are a kinesthetic tool children can use to frame in words within their guided reading selections. The frames bring their visual attention to whole words, parts of words, or even phrases. Emergent readers benefit from framing in important content words such as *caterpillar, pupa, butterfly* and discussing why these words are important to our understandings. I make the literacy frames from old file folders using the pattern that appears in *Snapshots* (Hoyt 2000).

FIGURE 5.4 A literacy frame in action.

Highlighter Tape

Highlighter tape is a semitransparent tape that students can use to "highlight" words that they believe are important, words that have a particular phonetic component, or words that they don't understand. It is reuseable and does not damage the books. Emergent readers really enjoy the tape as it makes the word turn the color of the tape.

FIGURE 5.5 Highlighter tape is used with *Fly Butterfly, Fly* (Newbridge).

Reading Glasses

Young children enjoy anything that feels dramatic and fun so I keep baskets of inexpensive sunglasses and eyeglass frames with no lenses in the reading center. Children are invited to change "reading glasses" as they enjoy re-reading guided reading selections. This supports re-reading for fluency and is a lot of fun as they discuss which pairs of glasses were the best! (I keep a container of antiseptic wipes and ask the students to wipe off the lenses before they begin reading.)

FIGURE 5.6 Star glasses.

FIGURE 5.7 Heart glasses . . . what's next?

RECOMMENDED FORMATS TO SUPPORT EMERGENT READERS

• Wall stories and class books provide a powerful link to nonfiction for emergent and developing readers.

• Supports within text generate an anchor of confidence and success as young readers approach nonfiction formats.

• Nonfiction books and articles often serve as a springboard for classroom activities that provide personal experiences.

• Various forms, text structures, and language features of nonfiction text are easily woven into wall stories and class books.

Darla Wood Walters is a K/1 teacher in Bend, Oregon whose language-rich environment is widely visited by teachers from many parts of the United States. She writes of the ways in which a language-rich environment and innovations on familiar texts can support the emergent learners by celebrating learning about the world while they learn to read.

Creating a Wall Story About Fruit Trees

Darla Wood Walters

I started by reading the nonfiction text *Seeds Grow Into Plants* by Mario Lucca, National Geographic, 2001. While this particular book was designed for guided reading, I chose to share it first as a read aloud since the concepts and content were ideal for all of my kindergarten students. As I began to read I encouraged prediction; participation was supported by students' prior knowledge, picture cues (photographs), patterning, and repetition in the language of the text.

The text pattern of this book reads:

These are apple seeds.
Apple seeds grow into apple trees.
Apples grow on apple trees.

Next, I brought apples, oranges, lemons, limes, watermelon, cantaloupe, and pumpkins into the classroom, providing personal experiences as each fruit was cut open. The seeds were examined, counted, planted, and the fruit was eaten!

With each fruit, the students joined me in a discussion surrounding the question of *What would grow from the seeds?* Would it be a vine, a bush, or a tree? Which items grow on trees and which ones on vines and bushes?

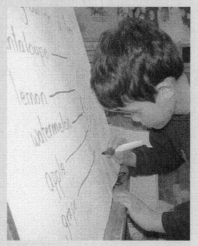

FIGURE 5.8 Darla and her students make a chart of their study.

FIGURE 5.9 A student fills in the chart.

We made a chart like the following to show what we were learning:

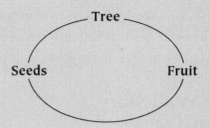

I have seeds. Do I grow on a tree?

cantaloupe ———— no

lemon ———————— yes

lime———————————— yes

pumpkin ——————— no

apple ————————— yes

orange——————————— yes

watermelon ————— no

Next, we produced illustrations using photographs, crayon, a dye wash, and dot stickers for the fruit and began to craft the text for our wall story. Please notice the index we included at the end of the wall story.

The pattern we chose is as follows:

◇ **The following wall story reflects information students gathered about our fruits with seeds that grow into trees.**

FIGURE 5.10

The following sample pages from our wall story reflects information students gathered about our fruits with seeds that grow into trees.

In this apple
is a seed

for an...   apple tree.

FIGURE 5.11 Students made these pages for our wall story.

In this lime
is a seed

for a...   lime tree.

FIGURE 5.12 Another student-made page.

Shared Reading

Once the wall story is constructed, it lends itself to shared reading, allowing children to see the message of the book as a whole, and providing them with support from their peers and teacher to tackle the text successfully.

FIGURE 5.13 Students read the wall story.

FIGURE 5.14 Reading the wall story is a valuable shared reading experience.

Notice the use of key supports within the text:

illustrations

personal experience

pattern and repetition

frequently used vocabulary

predictable story line

index

Additional text features we might have added to the wall story could include labels on their illustrations, captions below each picture, headings, a table of contents, and page numbers.

Independent Reading

The wall story provides an additional independent reading experience for young readers as they "read the room" with success and understanding while the teacher meets with small instructional groups for guided reading.

Class Book

As the text and story line become familiar to students, the wall story can be folded and stapled into the format of a class book. The class book is revisited during shared reading and provides familiar print for independent reading.

A rich literacy program includes fiction *and* nonfiction for all students, beginning at the most emergent stage. Students play with language, gain confidence, and learn about the consistencies of print. They begin to recognize and make use of formats and tools that are unique to fiction (i.e., speech bubbles, imaginary characters) and non-fiction (i.e., lists, photographs, an index). Creating a classroom of meaningful print with supports for understanding sparks the belief in children: "I can do this thing called READING"!

Generating Meaningful Print for Young Readers: The Informational Text Link

Darla Wood Walters

Wall stories and class books offer a fun, safe invitation to be a reader. Illustrations and print are often generated from hands-on classroom experiences, innovations on familiar Big Books, or connections with informational picture books. As the teacher controls the print to provide supports for successful reading, students develop a sense of ownership, creating illustrations and diagrams with a variety of art media. Print containing the following supports enables kindergarten and first-grade students to build confidence, skills, and strategies as they interact with print.

Supports for Successful Informational Text Experiences

illustrations that support the print	big, bold, minimal print
consistent placement on page	obvious spaces between words
appropriate length	predictable (simple) storyline pattern and repetition
topics relating to personal experience	rhyme and rhythm
familiar and natural language structures	fun use of vocabulary or print
frequently used vocabulary	
catchy introduction, clever ending	

6

Supporting English Language Learners
Building Content Knowledge and Language

Children of diverse language backgrounds have the same capacity for learning as all other children. Given appropriate school experiences and *time*, they can and do achieve at the same levels as their peers who are already familiar with the language of the school (Cummins 2000). While all children must develop the language of academic learning (CALP: Cognitive Academic Language Proficiency), English Language Learners (ELL) need learning opportunities with dual goals: content *and* language learning (Mohan 2001). This sounds simple but it must be remembered that it is not enough to immerse learners in content or to drop ELL children randomly into mainstream learning environments. They must have hands-on experiences related to the learning and have opportunities to engage interactively in conversation so that content and language develop hand in hand (Krashen 2000). The interactions that produce the greatest rates of both content and language acquisition are those in which learners have hands-on experiences and opportunities to activate prior knowledge *then* engage in speaking output with opportunities to clarify their intended meanings, even to reword what they are trying to say (Gibbons 2002).

This is vitally important as the dominant forms of conversations in classrooms often involve a teacher talking, then asking questions for which the answers are already known (Wong-Fillmore 1985). This kind of discourse does little to expand or elaborate upon language, and brain research would tell us it also has little impact on content learning. The teacher in this format is doing most of the work and the students are largely passive.

Strategies for Success

As we consider strategies to enhance learning with informational texts and stimulate language learning, some key points to consider might include:

Provide small group opportunities for ELL students. In small groups, students hear more language and have more language directed to them (Bruner 1978). Their output of language is also increased and there is more opportunity to clarify meanings.

Guided reading of informational texts. In guided reading, the content can be carefully scaffolded and language stimulated by the teacher. Content is supported through rich discussions, vocabulary supports, individual responsibility for engaging with the text, and reflections on both content and reading processes. A broader definition of guided reading may be necessary with ELL students as they will not necessarily always be reading the text as it was written. Emergent learners may use the informational photographs to stimulate language and content knowledge then craft their own text using comfortable language patterns. While this is a broader definition of guided reading, it will stimulate oral and written language proficiency while maintaining developmental supports for ELL students. Most importantly, the teacher is present to scaffold, extend, and support both content learning and language.

Partner pairs. While not as supported as guided reading, partner pairs increase learner responsibility, provide problem-solving opportunities, and offer a lower level of stress for ELL students with emerging levels of English language proficiency.

Cooperative groups. Cooperative groups usually operate without the immediate presence of the teacher but naturally include wonderful possibilities for language and content learning through shared responsibility and problem solving. The caution with ELL students is to structure your groups so that the native language speakers do not do all of the work and the ELL learner has equal opportunities to participate and to speak.

Jigsaw groups. A powerful extension to small group experiences may be a jigsaw-style format where students have opportunities to share their learnings with members of other groups. If each group read different resources on the same topic or engaged in a different scientific experiment, the sharing is a genuine interaction. Learners must attempt to clarify and express their meaning through language as their audience or partner did not have the same small group experience.

Present vocabulary in a meaningful context. Use pictures or real things whenever possible and use the vocabulary in multiple sentences and in multiple contexts. Try to use the words outside of the lesson in other situations and contexts.

Put vocabulary words on sticky notes. This way students can manipulate them around on the focus pictures, hold them in their hands to tell each other what they know, or place the sticky notes onto sheets of paper to draw their own illustrations related to the vocabulary.

Draw while you talk. Use stick figures, arrows, sketches to illustrate what you are saying.

Label pictures in books. See the following photograph with labels.

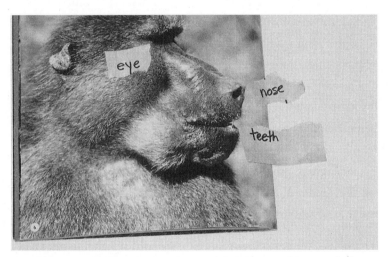

FIGURE 6.1 This page from *Baboons* is labeled to reinforce vocabulary (Dominic Press, 2001).

Encourage students to ask questions of the teacher and of each other. Record their questions and value them. ELL students respond especially well to generating questions about pictures as that gives them a strong context for the learning. To support this, I might ask them to preview the pictures in a book and think of questions. Their questions could be shared orally and written by the teacher, or students could write their own questions on sticky notes. This gives a frame into which their prior knowledge is naturally activated and content vocabulary begins to emerge.

Provide frequent opportunities for students to tell each other what they learned.

Focus on main ideas and write them down. Make the talk visible to the students. Connect main ideas to personal experiences and other readings whenever possible.

Use graphic organizers as visual supports to the content.

Encourage students to record their retells of content reading on tape. Save them as language development records, or for exemplary retells, make them available to other students to listen to the tape before they attempt to read the same passage.

Engage ELL students in higher-order thinking and problem solving whenever possible. Literal-level recall is too limiting to their cognitive development and does not synthesize language as effectively.

Encourage frequent stop points when reading informational texts. Use these stop points to reflect on what has been read, to talk about the content, to predict what is likely to come next, and so on.

Use student writing and dictation as guided reading material. By making photocopies of student-authored texts and using them as guided reading on informational topics, you expand the range of available texts for reading and ensure that the texts you are using match the oral language proficiency levels of your learners.

Use wordless information books such as the *Steps Into Windows Into Literacy* from National Geographic or the beautiful photographic friezes from Rigby and Newbridge to stimulate talk about content. Students can then dictate or write their own text to go with the pictures. Or, cover the words in books to encourage talk about pictures.

Give special attention to the visuals in a text before reading. Take time to look at all photographs, illustrations, charts, and graphs. Then engage the students in a discussion about the content. What do they think is happening? What do they already know about this? What words might appear on a page with this illustration?

In each guided reading lesson take time to talk about (1) What did we learn about _____ (*the content*) and (2) What did I learn about reading? How might I use what I learned about reading in my next book?

Teach note taking and sketching. When students stop to summarize their reading with a brief note or a quick sketch, they tend to remember more. The language cycles through their consciousness a second time and is more likely to be synthesized.

Engage in repeated readings of books. Re-read for different purposes. One reading might be for the main idea. A second reading to check for details on the life cycle of the butterfly. A third reading might be to look for descriptive words that helped you get a picture in your mind, and so on.

Consider cross-grade tutoring. This provides opportunities for ELL students to be reading partners with students both older and young than themselves.

Practice a variation on a barrier game. For example, after a guided reading experience on a topic such as butterflies, group students into pairs. One is the *teller* and one is the *illustrator*. The *teller* needs to describe a butterfly and the *illustrator* can only draw what the *teller* says. The *illustrator* cannot add information or details until the *teller* says he or she is finished. This really stimulates the *teller* to use clarifying and explicit language. The *illustrator* needs to really bolster listening skills. When the drawing is complete, the pairs return to the text to compare their work with the illustrations/photographs in the book.

Try *Tell It, First!* While turning the pages of a book, tell the students the content using a natural oral language-style discourse. Don't hesitate to add details and information that extend beyond the information in the text. You might also want to encourage learner questions as you move through the pages. Then, guide the students in reading the selection. (You might want to consider focusing this prereading experience in the learner's native language.) In either case, consider turning on a tape recorder to record your telling of the content. This tape, along with a tape of someone reading the actual text, can be placed with the book and made available for re-readings, revisiting the content, or for future students who need this level of prereading support.

Create wall stories. Post them and reread them often. See Chapter 5.

Create cloze activities with well-known texts. See Chapter 7 on skills and strategies.

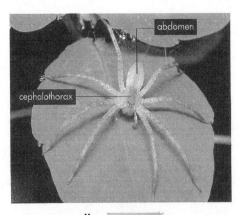

FIGURE 6.2 This cloze is from *Spiders* (Newbridge).

Retells

Teach Retells That Focus on Sequence

A poster with the following connectives can serve as a powerful stimulus for language expansion in retells. To use this, I demonstrate a lot of retells as we complete guided reading lessons, read alouds, and so on. In each retell I consciously use connectives in my retell. When I use each one, I point to the connective on the chart so it is clear that I am purposefully integrating these into my retell of the content. Soon, students are ready to begin working with partners. I give each person a sheet with the connectives listed and ask the pairs to retell the content for each other weaving in connectives as they seem appropriate. The students really like doing this and I find *the connectives weaving their way into their daily writing as well.*

CONNECTIVES

For Time	For Contrasting Ideas/Cause and Effect
First	On the other hand
Second	However
Third	Because
Then	As a result of
Finally	
Also	
In addition	
Plus	
After	

Teach Reflective Listening

I believe that learners need to be listen carefully to each other to encourage respect, language expansion, and content learning. To support that goal, I continually model active listening by giving direct eye contact to the speaker, leaning a bit forward toward the speaker, and then reflecting the speaker's language with statements such as: "I am hearing you say _____," "Would my summary of your statement be correct if I said _____," "So you are saying that _____," and so on. I model these behaviors carefully and make a point to tell the students what I am doing. My goal is to first heighten awareness of my reflective listening then to ask the students to engage in the same behaviors. When I believe they are ready, I ask one student to summarize a reading passage or offer an opinion on it and a second student to reflect back the message using a stem such as described previously. Soon, the students use these reflective listening practices as a natural extension of listening and as a segue into their own reflections.

Reflective listening seems to have a number of benefits to ELL students. (1) They feel that they have been respected and really heard when they hear someone reflect their ideas back to them. (2) If the message wasn't clear, they have an opportunity to clarify. (3) They listen more carefully to the language interactions of the group if they know they may need to reflect the content back in their own words.

Read, Cover, Remember, Retell

In 1999 I wrote about a strategy that had been created by Jan Ellison, a Title I teacher in my district. Since then *Read, Cover, Remember, Retell* (In *Revisit, Reflect, Retell*, Hoyt 1999) has assisted many children in reading more carefully and taking responsibility for consciously focusing on remembering information in text. The steps in *Read, Cover, Remember, Retell* include:

1. Find a partner.
2. *Read* about as much as you think you can cover with your hand.
3. *Cover* the text with your hand
4. Consciously focus on *remember*ing what you read. This is a quiet moment for thinking.
5. *Tell* your partner what you remember. (It is O.K. to peek back at the text if you need to.)
6. Read some more and follow the steps again.

Claudia Sanzone, reading specialist and Title I teacher at William Walker Elementary in Beaverton, Oregon, wrote the following to reflect how she and her ELL students took the process, personalized it, and made it their own!

Modifications to *Read, Cover, Remember, Retell*

Claudia Sanzone

I was teaching a group of third-grade ELL students strategies for comprehending nonfiction materials. I first modeled the *Read/Cover/Remember/Retell* strategy. This strategy asks students to read as much as their hand will cover. With their hand still over the text, they try to remember what they've read and then retell to a partner. If they forget, they can go back and sneak a peek. I always remind them that "rereading isn't a bad thing. Good readers do that all the time."

I had the students practice this for several days during our small group reading sessions with limited success. Since I wasn't getting the results I was looking for in terms of the students' ability to glean information from their reading, I added a piece to the strategy.

I modeled how to do a quick sketch at the end of each section of reading to collect my thoughts about what I understood. I also modeled how to do a quick word web.

So, now the steps are *Read, Remember, Represent, Retell*. The students tried this revised process by taking time to quickly sketch or word web after each chunk of text *before* telling their partner what they had learned.

Don't Stomp That Bug

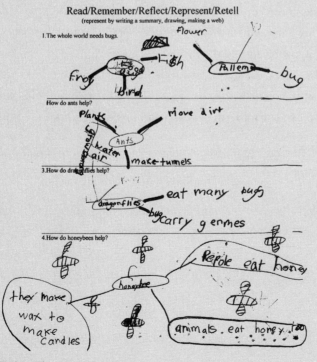

FIGURE 6.3 These samples illustrate the role of visual representation in supporting understanding.

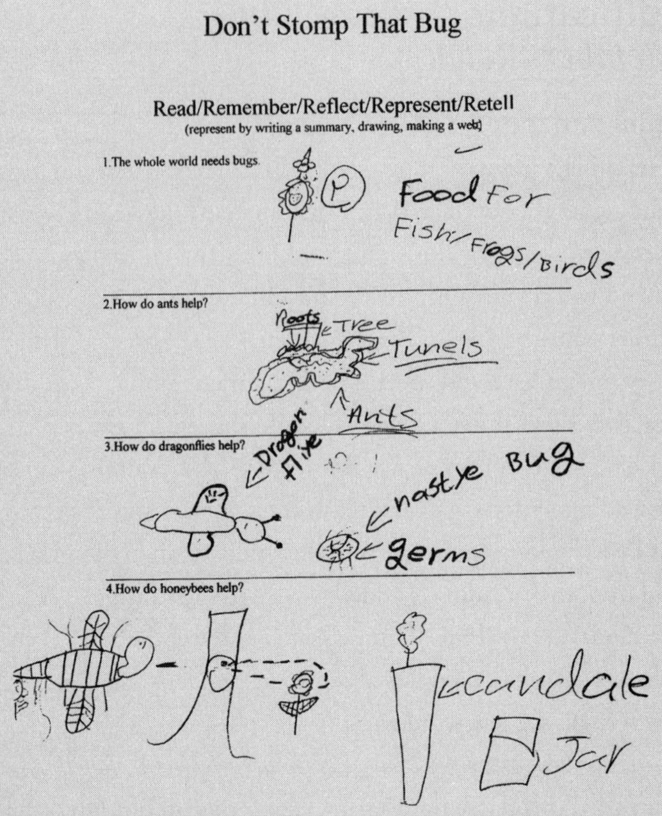

FIGURE 6.4 These samples illustrate the role of visual representation in supporting understanding.

The students became highly motivated and their level of understanding drastically increased. I was amazed at how accurately they were able to remember and retell some very detailed informational passages just by adding the *Representation* piece.

I am now using the revised process regularly and find that they can easily convert their understanding to written summaries as well. My ELL students love the process and feel very successful.

7

Teaching Reading Skills with Informational Texts

Informational texts are wonderful vehicles for teaching all of the skills we have traditionally taught in fiction during our "language arts time." Info texts support concepts of print, phonics, word knowledge, vocabulary, and grammar just as well as fiction! The more I have worked with info texts as vehicles for skills instruction, the more convinced I have become that the childrens' interest and curiosity about the topic make the skill easier to remember. As we have learned from brain research, learning is about making connections. When skills are infused into a topic of interest and related to a content area study, there are more points of connection for our learners to grasp.

In planning for skills teaching, I examine grade-level expectations for skill development, state standards, and my own beliefs about which skills are needed by this group of learners. Then, I look closely at the info text resources I am using in read aloud, shared book, guided reading, and content area studies to determine how a target skill might be demonstrated, practiced, and then assessed. I try to ensure that I am linking the target skill across many dimensions of the day to ensure adequate exposure to the skill. My goal is to demonstrate the skill repeatedly, treating it as an investigation, and provide students with ample opportunities to observe it in use (read alouds, shared books, modeled writings) as well as apply it in their own reading and writing (guided reading, content area reading, independent reading, guided writing, and independent writing).

Once the target skills for an age group are identified, I then utilize a chart such as Figure 7.1 which was originally published in *Snapshots: Literacy Minilessons Up Close* (Hoyt 2000). This enables me to look at unedited writing samples and identify which phonemes are being used in writing by each student. This is very important as I want to measure the sounds the learner can apply . . . not just recognize.

It is critically important that we stand accountable for learner development. Taking time to assess and then teach directly to areas of need is highly accountable teaching. Blindly following a program that provides instruction in a particular letter or sound without first assessing to see if the sound is needed by the student, or assessing only through flash cards and recognition-level tasks, may give us a clouded view of a child's actual needs. A phonic writing analysis takes very little time and has huge paybacks in terms of accountability and progress, especially for those learners most in need of our support.

As you can see from the chart that follows, this group of students is not yet using the letters *h, j, q, v, x, y,* and *z* in their writing. They may be able to recognize these sounds, but they are either not yet able to apply the sounds or have not had reason to use them in their writing. In response to what I have learned from the Phonic Writing Analysis, I could plan guided reading lessons that bring these particular sounds into focus for these students. This would allow me to further assess understanding and/or teach directly to those phonemes. After providing direct instruction, I would closely watch students' writing samples and daily reading for application of these target skills to determine if further instruction is needed.

Phonic Writing Analysis

✓ student analysis
( ) demonstration checklist

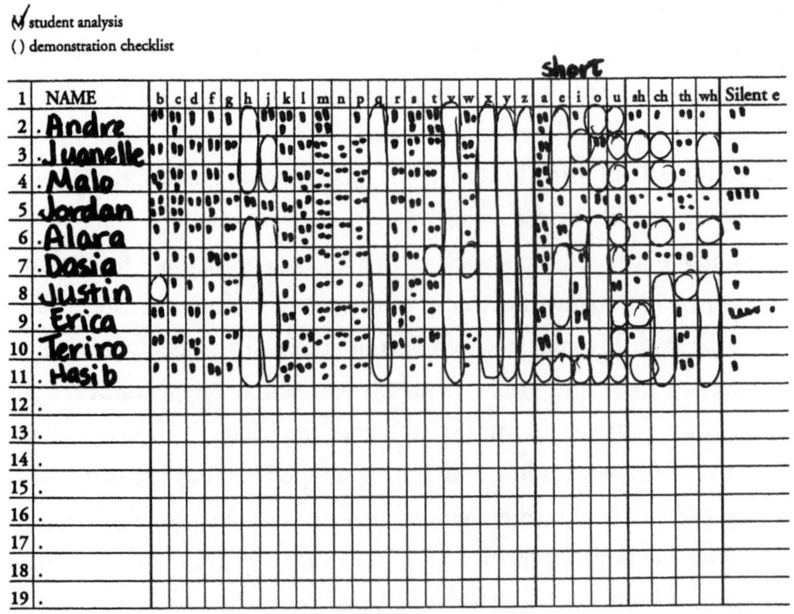

FIGURE 7.1 This analysis chart helps focus lessons on students' needs.

Phonic Writing Analysis

( ) student analysis
( ) demonstration checklist

NAME	b	c	d	f	g	h	j	k	l	m	n	p	q	r	s	t	v	w	x	y	z	a	e	i	o	u	sh	ch	th	wh	Silent e
1.																															
2.																															
3.																															
4.																															
5.																															
6.																															
7.																															
8.																															
9.																															
10.																															
11.																															
12.																															
13.																															
14.																															
15.																															
16.																															
17.																															
18.																															
19.																															

The following list of lessons are a sample of lessons meant to serve as springboards for your own thinking as you consider strategies for guiding students to assimilate essential reading skills while learning about the world.

Concepts of print

Initial consonants

Final consonants

Medial consonants

Consonant blends

Consonant digraphs (*sh, th, wh, ch*)

Long vowels

Silent *e*

Short vowels

R-controlled vowels

Structural endings: *-s, -ed, -ing*

Adding endings that cause a change in the spelling

Syllables: clapping, stretching, dealing with multiple syllables

Common rimes and onsets

Contractions

Compound words

Possessives

Conventions: capitols, periods, commas, question marks, semi-colons, colons, apostrophes, hyphens, dashes, parentheses

ei, ei rule

Parts of speech (nouns, verbs, adjectives, and so on)

Homonyms

Synonyms

Antonyms

Homophones

The lessons *you* design need to be based upon your observation of your students and upon the standards and curriculum from which you draw support. In all cases, our professionalism can stand at its highest level when we (1) observe our learners to gain a deeper understanding of the skills they have acquired and those that have not yet developed; (2) teach directly to those areas of observed need, using our observational data to guide our systematic instruction; and (3) monitor ongoing use of the skill in authentic writing tasks as use in writing is the truest measure of application-level understandings.

I Can . . .

My Name _____ Date _____

As you read this informational book, think about the strategies you are using. When you notice that you have used a strategy, tally a mark next to it and jot down the page number so you can tell someone what you did.

	Tally	Page numbers
When I read I can		
• Think about what makes sense		
• Look at the pictures		
• Use beginning sounds		
• Use ending sounds		
• Get my mouth ready to say the word		
• Find little words in big words		
• Read the sentence to think about what makes sense		
• Sound the word out		
• Chunk the word		
• STOP for a moment and think about what the author is trying to tell me		

Making an Informational Text Alphabet Chart

To support phonics instruction and make real-world connections, many teachers find that primary children benefit greatly from making their own class alphabet charts rather than depending on commercially produced alphabet charts. When alphabet charts are made with familiar and real-world materials such as leaves, grass, flowers, pencils, scissors, and candy bar wrappers children can use their world knowledge to relate easily to the letter/sound correspondences you are trying to teach. With some learners, Harry Potter stickers, photos of familiar characters from "Sesame Street" or "Disney" programs, ads from neighborhood stores with familiar logos such as Safeway, Albertsons, Kmart, CocaCola, Pepsi, McDonald's, and Burger King are meaningful. As you construct your class alphabet chart, make sure to leave room for photographs of students in your class. They love adding their photographs and names to the letter of the alphabet representing the first letters of their names. Be sure to post this at eye level rather than above your chalkboard so students can get close and really *use* the chart.

These homemade alphabet charts bridge language barriers, naturally activate world knowledge related to letter/sound relationships, and stimulate interest in the real world. For a powerful variation, you might consider having students make individual alphabet books with items from their own lives.

Making an Alphabet Book: Planning Page

I can make an alphabet filled with important things from my life. I can use photographs, illustrations, drawings, labels from my favorite foods . . .

A

B

C

D

continues

E

F

G

H

I

Making an Alphabet Book: Planning Page *continued*

J

K

L

M

N

continues

O

P

Q

R

S

T

U

V

W

X

Y

Z

Sample Phonics Lesson:
The Sounds of the Letter *G*

Gather a guided reading group together that needs work on the letter *g* according to the phonic writing analysis. Look closely at the *g* section on the class-made alphabet chart. Invite them to consider the real grass that they glued to the *g* section, and the pictures of *G*raciella and Ta*g*al. Next, you might revisit the labels for classroom components such as the *G*arbage can, *G*erbil, *G*lass on the window, Have *G*o cards in the writing center, and the Curious *G*eorge stuffed animal. These items could be grouped together and discussed in combination with reading letter *g* words on the word wall, in nonfiction Big Books, in environmental print, and so on. This rich and broad-based exposure to the sounds of the letter *g* doesn't need to be a precursor to guided reading. It is an extension and finetuning of the concepts of print and world knowledge students have been gaining through daily guided reading sessions. As this small guided reading group explores books such as *Wind and Rain* by Adria Klein, students can be challenged to watch closely for words using the letter *g*, then engage in a postreading discussion about the words they found and the different sounds made by the letter *g*.

The rain can be strong.
It can make the dirt move
down the hills.

The rain can be gentle.
It can make the grass green
and the trees grow.

8

FIGURE 7.2 This is a page from *Wind and Rain* (Dominie, 2001).

g words found	Hard g	Soft g
gentle		√
green	√	
grass	√	
grow	√	
strong	√	

Magnetic letters, wipe-off boards or Magnadoodles could be used to practice and solidify writing of these words as well as additional words using the letter g.

Lastly, students might review their writing folders to search for places where they have used the letter g in their writing or places where they could use words using the letter g to label a portion of a picture and expand on an idea in their writing for instance. By observing the use of letter/sound correspondences in reading and writing, and by treating word work as an investigation, we can ensure that our instruction is tightly matched to learner need and that readers are applying, not just naming, letters and sounds. This is not incidental instruction. It is planned, purposeful, systematic, and very tightly tied to learner phases of development.

Investigating Sounds

Name _____ Date _____

One of my jobs as a reader is to look for patterns in words. While reading for information, I am also looking for words with the pattern of

_____.

Examples found:

Word	Book	Page #

Student Observation Record
Word Solving Strategies in Informational Text

(for multiple observations over time)

Name of Reader _____

Observation 1   Date _____   Text _____

Observation 1   Date _____   Text _____

Observation 1   Date _____   Text _____

Observation 1   Date _____   Text _____

Observation 1   Date _____   Text _____

Observation 1   Date _____   Text _____

This student demonstrated the following word solving strategies while reading informational text: (Key: √ if behavior is observed)

	#1	#2	#3	#4	#5	#6
Uses initial consonants						
Uses ending sounds						
Checks medial sounds						
Chunks words						
Onset/rime						
Syllables						
Familiar parts						
Surveys the picture for clues						
Uses context clues						
Re-reads to regain meaning						
Re-reads for fluency						
Completes sentences to determine meanings of unknown words						

Reading with Scissors

Segmentation of print or "Reading with Scissors," a familiar fiction strategy, also works well in informational texts. As sentences and words are cut up, scrambled, and reassembled, students gain content knowledge, a sense of word order, and a strong focus on letter/sound relationships.

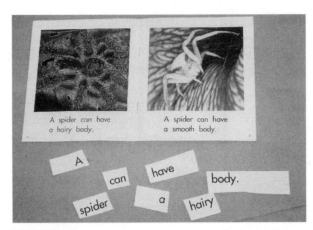

FIGURE 7.3

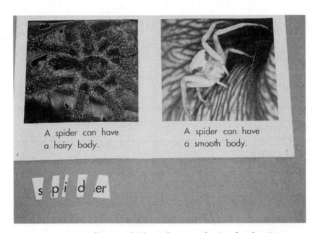

FIGURE 7.4 After guided reading with *Spiders* by Lisa Trumbauer (Newbridge Educational Books), students cut up individual sentences (Figure 7.3) and then cut up focus words into their component letters/sounds (Figure 7.4).

Using the Making Words Strategy with Informational Text

Pat Cunningham and Dorothy Hall (1999) popularized a strategy they call "Making Words." To connect this strategy to informational text, I survey an informational guided reading selection, textbook, news magazine, or other appropriate informational text for a word that is highly meaningful within this context and has linguistic features that would support a teaching point I want to make.

The main idea of the reading in the following passage is that insects and animals must elude predators in the rain forest. Animals with camouflage capabilities seem best suited to survival.

5 SURVIVAL IN THE RAIN FOREST

HIDE AND SEEK

There are insects everywhere in the rain forest, but sometimes it's hard to see them. To hide from predators, many use **camouflage**. They have bodies that look like leaves, lichens, or twigs.

Many of the hunters of the rain forest, like the jaguar and ocelot, also use camouflage. Their spotted brown, yellow, and black coats match the patterns of light and shade on the forest floor. This helps them creep up on their prey unnoticed.

When the morpho butterfly flies, it shows its brilliant blue wings, but when it lands, it seems to vanish. The underside of each wing blends perfectly with dead leaves.

This katydid looks like a leaf – it even has small holes to look as if insects have nibbled it.

The green chameleon is suited to life in the canopy. It moves very slowly and is hard to see among the foliage.

FIGURE 7.5 *The Living Rain Forest* by Nic Bishop (Pacific Learning).

I selected the word *predator* as a phonics follow-up to this very interesting informational passage. I chose it first because of its importance to the passage and secondly because this word supports investigations of three-syllable words and words with "-or" patterns that had been going on for some time with this group of students.

After reading and discussing the passage, I provide each student with a set of cards with the following letters, one letter per card.

e	d	r	p	a	s	o	t	r

We then begin to investigate letter patterns and word patterns that could be created with these particular letters. The students come up with two-letter words such as *to, as, Ed*; three-letter words such as *red, Ted, pot, rap,* and *dot*; four-letter words such as *soar, past*, etc. Whenever possible, I extend their thinking by pointing out common onsets and rimes, extensions that could be created by adding an ending such as *-ing*.

The process continues to build until a word that uses all of the letters is built (*predator*) and the students have a discussion about why I selected that particular word from the text. I ask them why was it important enough to earn this special attention?

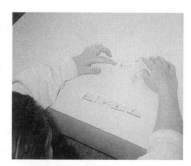

FIGURE 7.6 This is a sort with the word *soaring*.

Making Words Reflections

Name _____ Informational Text I Read _____

While I was working with the letters, the following are a few of the words I
made in each category.

2-letter words	3-letter words	4-letter words
5-letter words	6-letter words	7-letter words
words with more letters	Patterns I could make with these letters	

While building words I learned that . . .

This word was important to the topic we are studying because . . .

Assessing Word Solving Skills

Student _____ Date _____ Text Read _____

Target Word _____

Teaching Points Made in Session _____

This student was able to:

	Independently	With Assistance	Could Not Do
Create words with 2 letters			
Create words with 3 letters			
Create words with 4 letters			
Create words with 5 or more letters			
Change the beginning or ending sound to create a new word			
Separate an onset and rime			
Add an ending to change the base word			
Identify the syllables in the word			
Relate the meaning of the target word to the passage and explain its importance			

Additional Sample Lessons

Compound Words

Compound words are a target skill that I have selected. I explain to the students that we are going to investigate compound words. I make a chart and post it in a visible place. For a few days, I try to heighten sensitivity toward compound words by looking closely for them in nonfiction read alouds, shared book experiences, and content area reading. Each time I locate a compound word, I stop reading and think aloud about what the word means within the context in which I am reading. I then record the compound word and its meaning on the Compound Word Investigation Chart. As it becomes clear that the students are catching on, I ask them to help me continue the investigation by searching for compound words in their own nonfiction reading. Then, as they encounter compound words in the info texts used in guided reading, students are invited to add the words to our master chart, along with their meanings and the locations in which they were found.

Compound Word Investigation Chart

Compound Word	Meaning	Location Found
downdraft	Winds that push down toward the ground	*Storms*, Seymour Simon
hailstones	Ice pellets carried by wind	*Storms*, Seymour Simon
moonlight	Light from the moon	*Dogteam*, Gary Paulson
cobwebs	Webs spun by spiders	*Sign of the Beaver*, Elizabeth George Speare
wingspan	Width of bird's wings when outstretched	Science text
skateboard	A wheeled board	*Scholastic News*

Once I have guided the students in their investigation of compound words in a wide variety of reading texts, I shift to helping them investigate the role of compound words in their writing. A survey of their writing folders is a key step. As they re-read draft level and completed pieces, their goal is to search for compound words that may have appeared in their writing and also to look for opportunities to add compound words that might extend or elaborate on their message. During writing share, students can share the result of their personal writing surveys and discuss their observations. As a final level of assessment, I use a class list to record for each student my observations of their understanding as well as their use of compound words. To ensure success for all learners, I utilize a guided writing experience or an interactive writing experience for those students who are still developing an understanding of how compound words work.

With a process such as this, students quickly come to a far deeper level of understanding than they might have reached if I had simply asked them to complete a worksheet on compound words.

Grammar

During a guided reading segment with students who need support in understanding parts of speech, I guide the students in re-reading an informational passage to investigate nouns, verbs, adjectives, and so on within the passage. It is important to ensure that the passage has been read first for content so that their grammar exploration is occurring within a meaningful context.

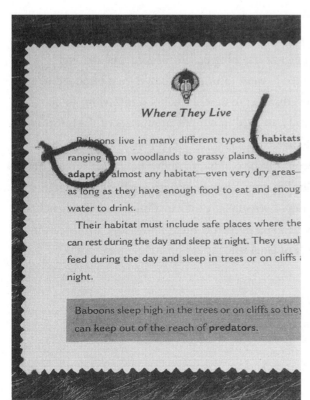

FIGURE 7.7

FIGURE 7.8 Notice how the students use Wikki Stix to identify parts of speech in Fig. 7.7 on page 5 of *Where Baboons Live* (Dominie, 2000) and in Fig. 7.8 on page 10 of *How Plants Survive* (Newbridge, 2001).

In a grammar lesson using *Where Baboons Live*, we started by re-minding ourselves of the differences between verbs and nouns, then started identifying the verbs on page 5 using Wikki Stix. To deepen content knowledge and to focus on quality of verb use, I then asked the students to identify the verbs that most accurately reflect key understandings about baboons. To accomplish this, they had to reflect on the content they had learned as well as the role the verbs had played in their developing understanding about baboons. The discussion made it very clear that all verbs are not equally useful to the reader and stimulated a powerful conversation about how writers might be more conscious of verb choice when communicating information.

VERBS	SUPPORT CONTENT KNOWLEDGE?	
	Yes	No
live	√	
can		√
adapt	√	
have		√
drink	√	
include		√

With this dual emphasis I am able to support grammar while still holding high standards for content area learning. Best of all, this kind of reflective grammar practice has a big benefit in students' writing!

The verbs selected as most informative could then be added to a class chart of action verbs used to describe baboon behaviors, to an alphabox (see page 271), or used in written summaries of the information learned about baboons.

Similar reflections can be conducted about nouns, adjectives, and adverbs. These fit flexibly into interactions with textbooks, resource books, news magazines—virtually any informational text! The benefits again, are doubled when you deepen content knowledge while learning about the finer points of language.

Cloze Lessons with Info Text

Cloze activities support a wide range of reader understandings while supporting content area knowledge. I often make transparencies of pages from nonfiction texts, cover key words with sticky notes, and then engage the students in a lively inquiry that requires them to use a wide range of strategies to determine the unknown words. If my goal is to support using context clues, then I cover the entire word. If my goal is to support beginning sounds, then I cut the sticky note to fit over all of the word except the beginning sound. If the goal is to use beginning and ending sounds, then I cut the sticky note to cover the middle portion of the word. This works well as a shared text experience for the whole class at the opening of a science lesson or a math lesson, and makes a powerful introduction to an informational selection during a guided reading session.

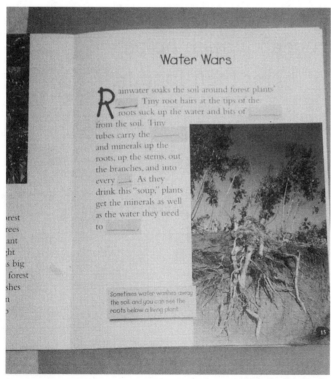

FIGURE 7.9 This is a cloze from page 15 of *How Plants Survive* (Newbridge, 2002).

Cloze Activities

Example #1 (Using context to determine unknown words)

Did you know that walruses, seals, and sea lions are all in the same animal _____? They love water and have bodies that are designed to make _____ easy. Their torpedo-shaped bodies slide smoothly _____ the ocean, which helps them to _____ for their food in the water.

Example #2 (Using meaning and beginning sounds to determine unknown words)

Did you know that walruses, seals, and sea lions are all in the same animal f_____? They love water and have bodies that are designed to make s_____ easy. Their torpedo-shaped bodies slide smoothly th_____ the ocean, which helps them to h_____ for their food in the water.

Cloze Activities

Example #4

Did you know that _alruses, seals, and sea lions are all in the same animal _amily? They love _ater and have bodies that are designed to make _wimming easy. Their torpedo-shaped _odies slide smoothly __ __ rough the ocean, which helps them to __unt for their food in the water.

Example #5 (Heightening awareness of verbs)

Hailstones begin to form when tiny particles of dust and ice collide with cold water droplets that freeze to them. Winds _____ these pellets around causing them to bump into more water drops and _____ even larger. As long as there is wind to keep them moving and cold water droplets to _____, the hailstones continue to expand getting larger and larger until they hit the earth.

Understanding Plurals

To support a linguistic concept with many rules to learn, such as plurals, I teach several minilessons, each focused on a different rule of pluralization. During each minilesson, I provide direct instruction in application of one rule and then engage the students in generating a list of words that use the rule. The lists are written on chart paper and then hung in the room in a visible place that is accessible to the students. I place a felt pen next to each chart and challenge the students to find more words that use each of the patterns while they are reading their informational texts. This heightens their awareness of the plural patterns and gives them opportunities to write content-related words on the charts, which enhances their content knowledge.

ADDING *S*

Book	books
Tree	trees
Dog	dogs
Horse	horses

ADDING *ES*

Fox	foxes

CHANGING *Y* TO *I* AND ADD *ES*

Body	bodies

CHANGING THE ENDING OF THE WORD

Cactus	cacti

THE WORD IS THE SAME, SINGULAR AND PLURAL

Fish	fish
Sheep	sheep

As students gain proficiency with the individual rules for creating plurals, I then challenge them in guided reading to watch for plural forms. For most students, this is best done during a second or a third reading of the text. I find that for many learners, searching for plurals or any linguistic pattern during a first reading is too distracting and detracts from their ability to focus on the content of the book.

I find that sticky notes cut into slim strips are great flags to mark words. Our discussion can then focus on which words they found and which rules of pluralization were applied.

The same procedure works well for verb tenses or any other highly functional rules of print.

Investigating Syllables

WORDS IN OUR DINOSAUR STUDY

1-syllable	2-syllable	3-syllable	4-syllable	5-syllable
bird	raptor	dinosaur	stegosaurus	tyrannosaurus
	reptile		amphibian	

WORDS IN OUR STUDY OF THE SOLAR SYSTEM

1-syllable	2-syllable	3-syllable	4-syllable	5-syllable
moon	planet	Jupiter		
sun	Neptune	telescope		
stars		asteroid		
Earth		gravity		

8

Where's the Door?
Finding a Path Through Informational Texts

Approaching Informational Texts: Finding a Path Through the Text

For the most part, readers need to approach informational texts differently than fiction. They need to shift their strategies to accommodate the focus on information rather than entertainment. They need to consciously think about remembering facts from their reading and to connect their path through a book to their purpose for reading.

To help make this clear to students, I bring in a collection of informational texts such as newspapers, recipe books, the manual to my car, a travel brochure, or a resource book with a table of contents. With the newspaper, I tell them how my husband and I read the paper in different ways. My purpose for reading the newspaper is to first learn about current events and secondly explore regional news. So, my newspaper reading will be focused on these two purposes. I make a reading plan in my head and I read the front section and the regional news first, then move to other sections as my time and interest allows. My husband, on the other hand, is most interested in sports so his strategies lead him directly to the sports page.

The same strategic thinking applies if I am reading my car manual to find out how to turn down the lights on my dashboard. I think about my purpose and decide if the table of contents or the index is more likely to help me find my answer quickly, then turn to the section that will provide the information the most quickly. My reading plan will be focused on finding the answer to a specific question.

My goal in thinking aloud through each of these kinds of informational texts is to make it clear that I start with a purpose. I have a reason to read the material. Then, based on my reason for reading, I pick and choose sections of each info text that I believe will match my purpose. This is a significant shift from reading fiction where you automatically start on page one and keep going until you are finished.

 11:00 a.m.

After studying the weather maps, the scientists decide conditions are right to produce a type of thunderstorm called a **supercell**. They know that tornadoes often come from supercells.

Characteristics of Supercell Thunderstorms

Strong **updrafts** (vertical winds with speeds up to 120 MPH)

Rotation (part of the thunderstorm is spinning)

FIGURE 8.1 Analyze these pages. Look at them as one visual image. Where would you start? Which text chunks support which visuals? What kind of a plan would best support reading of these two pages? From *Chasing Tornadoes* (Rigby).

Making a Reading Plan

Name _____ Date _____

Type of Informational Text _____

Work with a partner to examine a two-page layout in an informational text. As you look at these two pages, talk with your partner about how you would approach the reading. What would you do first, second, third? Would you read the pages in order? What parts of these pages would most help you activate your background knowledge? How might you use the charts and illustrations to help you?

First we would _____

Second _____

Third _____

Then _____

Try your plan and then talk about how well it worked for you. If you had another page like this would you read it in the same way? Is there anything you would do differently? _____

_____

What did you learn about the order in which you approach features such as headings, visuals, charts, and the text? How might this influence your informational writing? _____

_____

_____

Emergent Readers Need to Make Reading Plans

To set the stage for an exploration such as "Making a Reading Plan," I do lots of modeling and think alouds focused on the use of visuals, headings, and other supports to informational reading in Big Books. I want the students to be very clear about the conscious shifts I am making in my reading to accommodate the content demands of informational texts.

I *do not wait* until students are fluent readers or have arrived in the upper grades to provide these demonstrations and think alouds. I believe that we must expose emergent readers to an understanding of how strategies shift to match the texts we read and to ensure that they are spending significant amounts of time reading to learn. When children see reading as purposeful and interesting right from the start, we build an expectation that print is supposed to make sense. We help them to understand that reading brings you information as well as entertainment. We empower readers to make sense while they read.

With the youngest students, I demonstrate reading planning with Big Books, thinking aloud about illustrations, then pointing out headings and captions to show how they assist me as a reader. I engage students in helping me to check for features such as table of contents, index, and glossary. My purpose is to cast these features as tools for readers.

To make a reading plan, I serve as recorder while students do the thinking.

OUR READING PLAN

Our purpose for reading is _____

What we already know about this topic _____

We will begin by _____

Then we will _____

Next we will _____

We learned that _____

Over time, I guide these experiences through different forms of informational text. Emergent readers really enjoy seeing the strategies shift as we explore a menu, a how-to book, a book on an animal, or a recipe.

Linking Up to Guided Reading

During guided reading, the small group environment allows me to fine-tune, to closely observe emergent readers, and to assess how well the children are applying the planning strategies I have demonstrated.

During guided reading, we often return to one of our planning charts and wonder. Will the reading plan we made for a menu work in this book? Would the plan we made for a newspaper match? Do we notice features in this book that will help us make a plan that is just for this book? What do we do if the book doesn't have a table of contents? If we don't have a specific question in mind, will a picture walk help us think our questions? In our reading plan, did we remember to use the pictures to predict words that might appear on the page? Does our reading plan remind us to think about what we already know on the topic?

Emergent Reader: Informational Book Reflections

Name _____ Topic of This Book _____ Date _____

Before reading I remembered to:

☐ Think about what I already know on this topic

☐ Look at the pictures

☐ Ask myself questions about the topic

☐ Check for a table of contents

☐ Make a reading plan

While I read, I remembered to:

☐ Think about the topic

☐ Try to remember important ideas

☐ Use the pictures

☐ Think about what makes sense

☐ Look at the beginning sounds

☐ Point to the words with my finger

☐ Find a little word in the big word

☐ Ask myself if it sounds right

☐ Re-read sentences so they sound smoother

☐ Come back to tricky parts and try again

Learning to Shift Strategies

Name _____ Date _____

Select several informational resources that might include newspaper, magazine, recipe, directions, manual, brochure, or resource book. Consciously focus on your reading strategies. Try to notice the order in which you read parts of the texts, your purposes for each, and any other strategies you use.

TYPE OF TEXT	PURPOSE	STRATEGIES I USED IN THIS TEXT	PAGES READ
_____	_____	_____	_____
_____	_____	_____	_____
_____	_____	_____	_____
_____	_____	_____	_____
_____	_____	_____	_____

As I read these different kinds of texts and shifted my strategies to match my purpose for reading, I noticed that _____.

As I looked through these texts I found the ☐ visuals ☐ texts to be most helpful.

As I compare the way I read informational text to the way I read fiction, I notice that _____.

If I were to give advice to younger students about reading informational texts, I would be sure to tell them: _____

_____

_____

_____

Quick Reference Guide to Informational Text Strategies

This log is designed as a place where you can record think alouds and demonstrations your teacher completes with informational texts as well as observations you make in your own reading of information texts. The goal is to create a reference tool you can use to quickly remind yourself of the most efficient strategies for reading different kinds of texts.

Text Type	Strategies to Use	Reflection from My Reading	Comments
(directions, newspaper, textbook, article)			

Reflecting on Comprehension Strategies

Balancing Explorations in Fiction and Informational Texts

It is essential to identify which comprehension strategies students can utilize in both fiction and nonfiction. Strategies such as prediction of text structure, activation of prior knowledge, self-questioning, making connections, shifting reading rate, inferring, visualizing, and summarizing can be highly useful across many genres.

To ensure that I am assisting students in this important understanding, I have begun to keep a record of think alouds to monitor the balance of my comprehension demonstrations in fiction and in nonfiction. My goal is to ensure that learners understand key comprehension strategies and can flexibly implement them across many kinds of texts.

Good Readers of Informational Text

- Have clear goals for their reading
- Look over the text before reading, notice illustrations, headings, charts, etc.
- Activate prior knowledge
- Make predictions
- Use meaning and expect the text to make sense
- Understand whether or not comprehension is occurring
- Make connections: text to self, text to text, text to world
- Create visual images
- Consciously use text features (pictures, headings, captions, boldface type)
- Draw inferences, conclusions
- Ask questions as they read
- Read different kinds of informational texts differently
- Skim and scan to recheck information
- Locate information
- Adjust reading rate to match the demands of the text
- Make a plan when reading informational texts
- Identify important ideas and words
- Consciously shift strategies to match purpose
- Retell, summarize, synthesize
- Use a variety of fix-up strategies
    - √ Read on
    - √ Backtrack
    - √ Context clues
    - √ Make substitutions
    - √ Look at word parts: beginnings, endings, chunks

This was adapted from the work of Pearson and Duke 1999; Keene and Zimmerman 1996.

Adjusting Reading Rate in Informational Texts

Good readers adjust their reading rate to match the demands and the tone of the text being read. We might utilize a fast reading rate for a Shel Silverstein poem to enjoy the lively language or speed things up as we get to an exciting moment in *Hatchet*. In informational texts, we often need to read at a slower rate to give ourselves time to ponder the information; time to make connections and to determine important ideas as we read.

To support that understanding, I engage students in doing some research on times good readers read fast and times they read more slowly. We research by wondering about the rate in different kinds of read alouds, in newsmagazines, in the math textbook, and so on. We wonder about approaching a textbook passage with a really fast scan followed by a slow and deep reading.

The goal is to heighten sensitivity about reading rate and to ensure that learners do not use just one rate of speed for all texts and all purposes.

WHEN TO READ FAST	WHEN TO READ SLOWLY
Shel Silverstein Poems	Dramatic pieces
When skimming	When reading details
Searching for a particular point	Making connections

Inferring in Informational Text

Good readers make inferences. As they read they make connections to what they already know, other texts they have read, and their knowledge of the world. They use those connections to infer information that isn't directly stated in the text. Inferential reasoning is regularly taught in fiction, but we very much need to infer in nonfiction texts as well. Children grow up making inferences about the real world such as, "That dog is wagging his tail and looks really friendly. I think I could pet him and not be bitten." Or "Hmm. Mom looks like she is really busy, I think I will wait until later to interrupt her."

Students need to understand that we make inferences in informational texts just as we do in fiction, so we practice. We practice making inferences from body language, from photographs of ourselves and our families, from predictable books, and with sentences such as:

The ambush bug stays perfectly still as it waits for another insect to land. (From *True Bugs, When is a Bug Really a Bug?* By Sara Swan Miller, Franklin Watts, 1998.)

WE CAN INFER THAT	SUPPORT IN THE TEXT
the ambush bug is patient.	This inference is supported by the statement "stays perfectly still."
the ambush bug is a predator.	"waits for another insect to land."

With adequate modeling, readers can infer from even so little as a sentence and experience the power of reading beyond what is stated.

Making Inferences in Informational Text

Reader _____ Text _____ Topic _____

I CAN INFER THAT	MY INFERENCE IS BASED ON	THE PICTURE	THE TEXT

Drawing Conclusions

When readers draw conclusions from their reading, it is much easier to make generalizations and determine important ideas.

Reader _____ Text _____ Topic _____ Date _____

Facts from my reading:

_____

_____

_____

_____

Conclusions I can draw include:

_____

_____

_____

_____

I believe the very most important ideas are:

_____

_____

_____

Self-Questioning Strategies

Reader _____ Text _____ Date _____

My questions about this topic	Answers found in text	Pg #	I still wonder about

The following chart titled Comprehension Strategies Log could be a class record of comprehension strategies demonstrated in informational text or a personal log of reflections. (Focus on self-questioning, inferring, identifying important ideas, visualizing, summarizing, predicting, using text features.)

Comprehension Strategies Log

Reader _____

TEXT(S) READ	COMPREHENSION STRATEGIES USED	WHAT I LEARNED ABOUT MYSELF AS A READER OF INFO TEXTS

Jodi Wilson, Early Childhood Facilitator and Staff Developer in Spokane Schools, Spokane, Washington, offers the following reading chart as a tool for students and educators to consider in reflecting on the shifting stances we take as readers. Please notice in the chart the reference to a reader's "gateway" into the text (Moline 1995). This is of critical importance as in fiction the gateway is always the beginning. In informational texts, the gateway for a reader can occur at almost any point that matches the reader's interest and purpose.

The Different Ways Readers Approach Different Kinds of Text

Jodi Wilson

	Reading for "Story"	Reading for "Information"
Purpose for Reading	Usually for Pleasure	Combination of Enjoyment and Learning
Way in which text is read	WHOLE text—front to back, top to bottom, left to right	May read only PART of the text
	Pick up reading where we left off	Pick up book and begin reading in an entirely different place for an entirely different purpose
	To gain the greatest meaning, pages need to be read as arranged and in sequence	Visual information might be read bottom to top, right to left, circular, back to front, or in a zigzag fashion depending on design and purpose for reading
Gateway (where a reader chooses to enter the text)	The first line of the text	Gateway varies. Could be: • the table of contents • the index • headings and subheadings • the pictures and captions
Visual elements	Verbal narrative does not necessarily need pictures to make meaning	Visual information (photos, maps, diagrams, etc.) can be read for meaning even with few or no words Words may have little or no meaning with diagrams or other visual elements

This table was adapted from *I See What You Mean: Children at Work with Visual Information*, Steven Moline, Stenhouse, 1995.

9

Prereading Strategies
Building Understanding for Content and Vocabulary

Frontloading

To improve understanding and scaffold vocabulary in informational texts, I always attempt to *frontload* vocabulary and concepts so the reading is fully supported by understanding. My goal is to provide rich dialogue and experiences using the vocabulary of the text *before* reading. If I engage students with real experiences using vocabulary in the same context in which it will be read, I increase the learners' confidence with both the vocabulary and the content. When frontloading informational texts, you:

- learn about something
- talk about it
- wonder about it

Then, read about it using the concepts and vocabulary that have been frontloaded before approaching the text.

This process naturally brings prior knowledge to a level where it is ready to apply, stimulates questions on the topic, builds interest, and most of all builds the content language that will support the reading.

Many textbook publishers still offer teaching suggestions that include listing vocabulary on the chalkboard, looking it up in the index or glossary, and so on. While these activities may assist students who already possess prior knowledge on a topic, struggling students with limited prior knowledge are left without concepts to support their reading and are more likely to have difficulty in creating meaning while reading.

Planning for Frontloading

To plan a lesson that utilizes frontloading, I try to first think in terms of the concepts a reader needs to understand to interact meaningfully with a text. Whenever possible, I attempt to ground those concepts and the language that surrounds them in real experiences.

For example, before attempting to read about *magnets*, I would engage students with real magnets. As they try to identify what a magnet will or will not pick up, learners generate questions, discuss prior experiences with magnets, and naturally use language to describe their observations. As the experience continues, I might ask students to generate words about magnets so I can list them on chart paper or the overhead or ask learners to work with a partner to generate as many words as they can related to what they are seeing. (Alphaboxes work well for this. Please see Chapter 18.)

To support technical vocabulary that is not appearing naturally in their exploration with magnets (words such as *polarization*, *North Pole*, and *South Pole*), I demonstrate how polarization works with bar magnets and give the students a chance to experience the pulling and pushing action. The next step is to add words like *poles* and *polarization* to the word lists or alphaboxes they have been creating.

WORD LIST FOR MAGNETS

pick up

pull

paper clip

pins

horseshoe

bar

stick together

large

small

heavy

light

metal

plastic

bolts

North Pole

South Pole

polarization

With ELL students and others who need additional scaffolding of language and content, I might have them *write* about magnets using as many of the magnet words on the chart as they can. This provides an additional experience with both the content and vocabulary so the language is fully internalized.

What can a magnet pick up?

A magnet can pick up paper clips.

FIGURE 9.1 A page from *Magnets* (Newbridge).

Thanks to the supports provided by frontloading, the vocabulary of the text is now familiar, well-rooted in concepts and real experience and is easily remembered. If I had started with the text and not taken time to engage with the real magnets, students who had previous experience with magnets would have read with understanding. Students with underdeveloped English or limited experience with magnets would have been in danger of just decoding without real understanding.

Frontloading News Articles

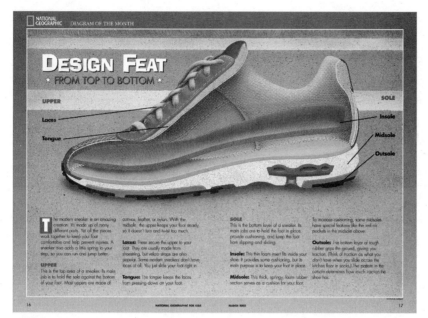

FIGURE 9.2 These pages are from *National Geographic for Kids*.

To frontload this article, I start with a discussion of tennis shoes or sneakers worn by students in the class. Volunteers remove a shoe and place it on a desk while team members try to label the various portions of the shoe's construction. A list of component parts (*upper, laces, tongue, sole, insole, midsole, outsole*) is placed on the chalkboard while students are challenged to find each of those components in the shoe on their desk. Teams also discuss, draw, and write about the function of each component part. What does it do and why is it important?

Next, I provide a list of words that I know are in the text and I want to ensure are read with meaning. My challenge to the students is: *The following words and phrases are in this article about shoes. Work with your team to discuss how you think these words and phrases might be important in an article about sneakers.* (Focus words and phrases: *prevent injury, comfortable, creation, canvas, leather, nylon, rubber, velcro, modern, pressing, layer, cushioning, foam insert*).

This discussion grounds the vocabulary firmly within the content and gives the students opportunities to use the vocabulary in oral conversation before engaging as a reader, which strengthens their understanding of the meaning. This also ensures that there will be multiple interactions with the vocabulary as the students will first see the words/phrases in a list, next they will talk about them, then they will read them.

Now the students are ready to read with meaning. They will have a secure understanding of the content, multiple experiences with the vocabulary, and have encompassed the vocabulary into their oral language bank as well.

Prereading Vocabulary Focus

Reader _____   Date _____

Title of Article _____   Topic _____

Topic-related words I think might appear in this article

_____ _____ _____ _____

_____ _____ _____ _____

_____ _____ _____ _____

FOCUS WORDS/PHRASES PROVIDED BY THE TEACHER	BEFORE READING I THOUGHT THIS WAS IMPORTANT BECAUSE	AFTER READING I THINK

Words/phrases I think are important:

In general, for emergent readers and vulnerable learners (Batzle 2002), I provide as much frontloading as I possibly can and attempt to keep experiences with informational text as close to their life experiences as possible. For students who reach higher levels of proficiency as readers, who have well developed academic language for content area reading, and who have a range of metacognitive strategies for dealing with informational text, I can somewhat reduce the frontloading and move to more abstract concepts that are further removed from their life experiences. I will not, however, totally remove frontloading in instructional materials as we know that all readers, even adults, benefit from a preview of a text, time to connect to background knowledge, and time to talk about what they read.

In the book *Egypt* (National Geographic), frontloading might begin with the introduction, followed by a discussion centered around questions such as: What do you already know about Egypt?

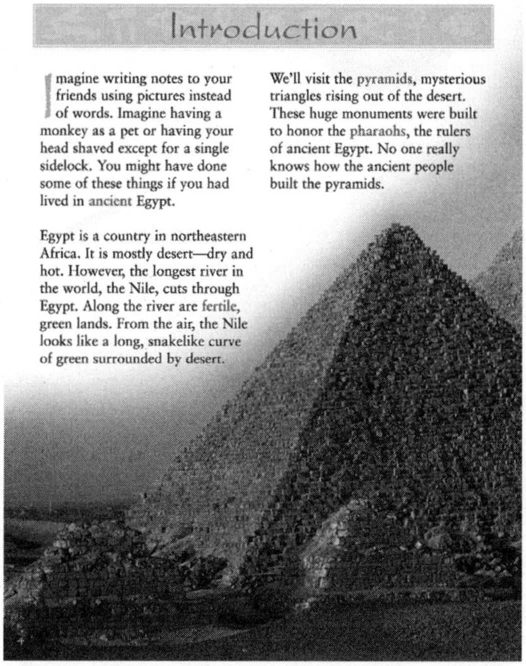

Introduction

Imagine writing notes to your friends using pictures instead of words. Imagine having a monkey as a pet or having your head shaved except for a single sidelock. You might have done some of these things if you had lived in ancient Egypt.

Egypt is a country in northeastern Africa. It is mostly desert—dry and hot. However, the longest river in the world, the Nile, cuts through Egypt. Along the river are fertile, green lands. From the air, the Nile looks like a long, snakelike curve of green surrounded by desert.

We'll visit the pyramids, mysterious triangles rising out of the desert. These huge monuments were built to honor the pharaohs, the rulers of ancient Egypt. No one really knows how the ancient people built the pyramids.

FIGURE 9.3 Abstract concepts and understandings need to be frontloaded *before* reading begins. This page is from *Egypt* (National Geographic).

What mental images did you get as you read? Which three words in this passage do you think are important enough that we are likely to see them again while reading about this topic? Why? If you were to quickly draw a sketch showing the landscape of Egypt, what would you include? Could you show on a map of the world where Egypt is located? What do you know about that portion of the world? What do you know of the following words: *pyramids, monuments, pharaohs, ancient, Nile, sidelock, Africa, fertile*. Why do you think these might be important to our study of Egypt?

Prereading Discussion

Topic _____   Read page _____ and be prepared to discuss.

What do you already know about _____?

As you read page _____, what did you think about? _____

_____

_____

Find two places in the text where you got a very clear visualization. What was in your mental picture? _____

_____

_____

What connections were you able to make? _____

_____

_____

List at least three words you believe are important to this topic and that we are likely to see again as we read further. Tell why you chose them. Are there any words that weren't used in this passage that you think will be important to this study?

_____   _____

_____   _____

_____   _____

List words you wondered about, even if you aren't sure of their meaning.

_____   _____   _____

_____   _____   _____

_____   _____   _____

List your questions about this topic.

_____

_____

_____

Crafting Texts Before Reading

To stimulate language and vocabulary, I often use sticky notes to cover the text block on pages of text, then engage students in a discussion designed to elaborate their understanding and bring out the language of the printed page. This can be supported by having students create labels for the pictures and by writing their own text for the page. Once they have crafted their own texts, they can remove the sticky notes and compare their work to that of the author.

FIGURE 9.4

FIGURE 9.5 Notice how sticky notes covered the original text to allow room for student-generated text. Labels have been added to the photograph to support vocabulary. After writing their text, students remove it to compare to the original.

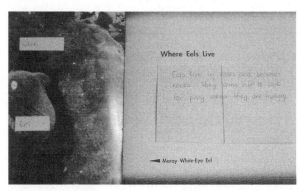

FIGURE 9.6 The same process was followed as above: Lots of conversation followed by labels on photographs, students writing their own text, reading the author's version, and discussing.

Prereading Picture Sorts

Newbridge Discovery Links provides blackline masters called *Home School Connections* that are designed to provide photocopy-ready take home versions of guided reading selections enjoyed at school. I have found these Home School Connections to be powerful for prereading as well. As you can see in the picture below, students can arrange the pictures in an order that makes sense to them, add labels to the picture, and create a text either through teacher dictation or their own writing. When they read the original text in the matching guided reading book, they can celebrate how much they think like an author!

FIGURE 9.7 Eric and I sort photographs and then match text blocks to the appropriate pictures.

Word Theater

Word theater engages students in pairs using charades-style interactions to act out key vocabulary before reading. The words, phrases, or concepts are selected by the teacher from a text students will soon be reading. The students have to apply their prior knowledge and often talk to each other about unfamiliar concepts to enable them to dramatize the vocabulary. They enjoy the body movement and really reach deep as they try to grasp the concepts as well as consider options for making it clear to their observers as the word theater begins. This can become a gameshow-style experience if the words as posted on a chart and observers need to guess which words are being dramatized.

After reading, students can use word theater to act out words and phrases they considered to be highly important to the topic.

Word Prediction

Have students preview the pictures in a text then work with a partner to predict topics related to the words they think they will encounter while reading.

Wheel of Fortune

Like the game show on television, blanks are created for each letter in a statement or phrase related to the reading passage. Before reading, students need to look at the clues and try to puzzle out the words or phrases. I observe closely and provide letter clues, picture clues, and meaning clues as needed.

___ ___ ___ ___ ___ ___ ___

CLUE: Line 1. What is this book about? (Answer: magnets)

___ ___ ___ ___ ___ ___ ___ ___ ___ ___ ___

CLUE: Line 2. What can magnets do? (Answer: Pick up bells)

After students have solved the puzzle, they love reading the text and comparing.

M ___ ___ net

Be ___ ___ s

A magnet can pick up bells.

FIGURE 9.8 A magnet can pick up bells.

Prereading Word Sorts

For a prereading word sort, I preview the text and select an array of words and phrases that I believe are important to understand. I try to ensure that half to two-thirds of the words are familiar to ensure success.

SAMPLE WORD SORT FOR EAGLES

soars	skillful	fierce hunter
wingspan	bird of prey	prevent spread of disease
predator	large eyes	sees eight times more clearly than humans

1. I arrange the words and phrases onto an 8 × 11 sheet of paper and ask the students to separate them onto rectangles that can be easily moved.

2. Partners match up words and phrases into pairs that seem to go together and then make a statement that uses the target vocabulary.

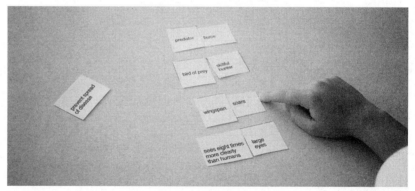

FIGURE 9.9 *Wingspan* and *soars* could turn into: The broad wingspan of an eagle allows it to soar for long distances.

3. As they gain proficiency, I have students group words and phrases into threes and again make statements.

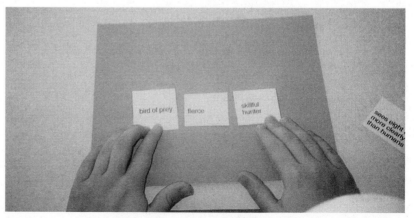

FIGURE 9.10 These three cards turned into: Birds of prey are fierce and skillful hunters.

4. Students are now ready to read the passage. I ask that while they read, they be thinking about the words and phrases they worked with during the sort. As they find each one in the text, their job is to stop reading, consider the word or phrase in the context of the whole passage, and then continue reading.

FIGURE 9.11 Focusing on important words and phrases *during* reading.

If they have words and phrases left over when they finish reading, they need to re-read to try to find the ones that were missed.

Skimming for Important Words Before Reading

I often have students skim a text to search for words they believe may be important before they actually settle into detailed reading. You could have them use Wikki Stix, which are waxed yarn strips, to mark words they found during their prereading survey, sticky notes, or just make a list. Words can also be listed in journals, on charts, or in any format that fits your classroom and age of the students.

Life on the Move

People who move around a lot are called nomads. The Navajo Native Americans used to be nomads. Their traditional home is a hogan, which means "home place." A hogan is a simple house made from logs and mud. It's built in the shape of a dome.

Hogans are very important to the Navajo. They hold a special ceremony when a new hogan is built. They believe that this protects them from danger and illness.

There are many kinds of hogans. They are all built in different ways.

The forked-pole hogan was the first hogan to be built.

The log-roof hogan is bigger than the forked-pole hogan. It was built to give families more room.

FIGURE 9.12 Students skim to try to capture important words before reading.

I find that when students take time to skim the text for important words, they naturally pick up boldface words, words in topic sentences, and words in titles. If they are catching the most important words so we can discuss them, great! If they are not, then I try to do more modeling of how to skim for key words as well as return to more frontloading of content so they have a stronger idea of the big ideas related to this unit of study.

Amy Goodman, a middle school teacher in Anchorage, Alaska, used prereading word sorts in fiction and in nonfiction and writes the following:

Word Sorting

Amy Goodman

I decided to try your word sorting activity in my eighth grade language arts classroom last week. I wanted to let you know how effective it was getting kids to think about the vocabulary words they would encounter in a story we were going to be reading. I used the same grid format you shared during the inservice. I decided to only make one copy for every two students to save paper and time in cutting them apart. I loved the collaborative nature of this activity in that it got my kids talking to one another about their prior knowledge of the words. Because the students were challenged to sort the words into categories, they had to first work out the meanings of the words. Of course, they didn't necessarily know all of the words I had put in front of them, but by working in tandem they knew more than they would have on their own.

I then had them shift gears and challenged them to try putting pairs of words together to formulate sentences. We shared these orally and it was so interesting to hear how the students took different approaches with the various meanings of the words. That heightened their interest, which improved their comprehension of the story when we finally read it. The kids told me they were subconsciously on the lookout for those words as they read.

Another plus to the word sort activity was how these cut-up words conveniently turned into flashcards. Students recorded definitions on the back and used them as traditional flashcards before taking the final test on this story.

I really think the success of these word sorts is the tactile approach (the cutting, the shuffling, the sorting) and the fact that kids worked collaboratively. Lots of excellent learning went on, and I know I will use these again.

10

Taking Time to Wonder
Questioning Strategies
to Build Comprehension

I used to believe that I was teaching comprehension when I carefully asked readers questions. Sometimes those questions came from a teacher resource guide, sometimes I generated the questions myself, but rarely were these the questions of the learners.

I realize now that student-generated questions are vital to comprehension. They give us a window into the thinking of the reader, a sense of the level of prior knowledge on the topic, and offer a measure of insight into student interests. Best of all, they deepen learner understanding (Pearson and Duke 1999; Keene and Zimmerman 1997).

When learners ask questions before, during, and after reading they learn more. Student-generated questions build intrinsic motivation for reading, have an established purpose for reading, increase personal connections, and stimulate higher-order thinking (Hoyt 1999). Questioning is especially effective in informational texts as it helps students to better understand the research process, which forms the infrastructure of informational texts.

FIGURE 10.1 Even emergent readers can engage in questioning strategies.

To make the process clear to students, I model questioning in all areas of the curriculum and encourage the students to verbalize their own wonderings. As I model, I try to consciously utilize a wide range of questioning styles and topics.

BEFORE-READING QUESTIONS/REFLECTIONS:

I wonder what this will be about . . .

I wonder how the author has organized the information . . .

I wonder what visual supports the author has provided. I think I will look through the pages.

If I could talk to the author, I would like to ask why there is a question at the beginning of each paragraph.

I wonder if the author will . . .

I have always been curious about _____. I wonder if that will be covered in this passage.

As I look at this page, I realize I don't have much experience with this topic. I really wonder about . . .

I hope the author will talk about . . .

I really want to know about . . .

DURING-READING QUESTIONS/REFLECTIONS:

I'm not sure what this word means. I am going to finish the sentence to see if I can figure it out.

I wonder if the next page is about the caterpillar's cocoon. This page is about the caterpillar eating and I know that they eat before they spin a cocoon.

I don't understand this. I wonder what the author is trying to say?

As I look at the picture, I really wonder about . . .

I really wonder what this meant. I am going to read it again to try to make sense of it.

This is really interesting. I wonder how the writer made me feel so excited!

AFTER-READING QUESTIONS/REFLECTIONS:

The author didn't cover _____. I wonder where I could learn more about that.

This made me really curious about . . .

I wonder about the author's message. I think it was . . .

If I were to pick three main ideas, they would be . . . I wonder what the author wanted me to understand?

- My favorite part was . . . I wonder which part the author liked best?

- What did you like the best?

- Which ideas did you think were the most important?

- I wonder why the author chose this style of writing to share the information?

- Could a poem have covered this? Could I turn this into a story?

Scaffolding Reader Questions

I support the before-, during-, and after-reading questions of students by encouraging them to verbalize and record their questions. With emergent learners, I act as their secretary to record their questions. With more fluent readers, I encourage them to record their questions individually or in teams.

Emergent/Developing Reader Example: Elephants

BEFORE READING

Based upon my preview of	*My questions are*
Title and table of contents	What does the elephant eat?
Pictures	Will this book tell about their food?
Diagram	How does the trunk have bones?

DURING READING

While I was reading I noticed	
The elephant ate some hay.	What else do they eat?
The baby was right by the mother's feet	Do they ever get stepped on?

AFTER-READING QUESTIONS

I still wonder about the bones in the trunk.

I want to know why the author put a picture of the baby on a page where she talked about where the elephants live.

Fluent Reader Example: Decline of Native American Cultures

BEFORE READING

Based upon my preview of	*My questions are*
Title and table of contents	Why did the author try to cover such a wide range of topics?
The boldface headings	What is the author's main idea?

The chart on page 16

Why did the culture decline so rapidly?

DURING READING

While I was reading I noticed

"The diseases introduced by the European settlers spread quickly through the Native Americans."

Was this one reason for the rapid decline in population or was it also gradual loss of hunting grounds?

The population graph on page 19 shows that the rise in European Americans matched a drop in Native American population.

Why do they match?

After-reading questions

After reading I realize the author tried to cover too many topics and did not give enough information. Why did the author do that?

I feel that I need to know more about issues related to the spread of disease in the Natives and the expansion of Europeans into abandoned Native American villages.

Questions	Answers	Interesting Details
How do they go up a really steep part and not fall backwards?	Because they have a electric motor and a chain that's helping it up.	In 1976, no roller coaster featured loops.
How do they go down and not hit the bottom and crash?	Because the kinetic energy	A loop is not a perfect circle, because if it was the roller coaster would be at such high speeds that humans would be passing out.
How do they go upside-down and not fall off?	Because of the gravitation	There are 3 sets of wheels.
How does the engine work?	rides use a chain powered by an electric motor	You're not always on a chain

FIGURE 10.2 When students record their questions, and consciously notice as answers are gathered, they think more deeply about the topic.

Developing Guiding Questions Before Reading

Name _____ Text _____ Date _____

Before-Reading Questions

Based upon my preview of   My questions are

_____   _____

_____   _____

_____   _____

_____   _____

During Reading

While I was reading I noticed

_____

_____

_____

_____

After-Reading Questions: I still wonder about . . .

_____

_____

_____

Assessment of Question Quality

Assessment completed by _____ (teacher)

Student _____ Date _____ Focus Text _____

This student's before-reading questions reflected	(1) Minimal– (5) Substantial
• Use of the title and visuals	1 2 3 4 5
• Connections to prior knowledge	1 2 3 4 5
• Interest in the topic	1 2 3 4 5
• other _____	1 2 3 4 5

The student's during-reading questions reflected

• Citations from content	1 2 3 4 5
• Use of prior knowledge	1 2 3 4 5
• Critical thinking	1 2 3 4 5
• Information from text and visuals	1 2 3 4 5
• other _____	1 2 3 4 5

The student's after-reading questions are

• Reflective	1 2 3 4 5
• Evaluative	1 2 3 4 5
• Extend beyond the text	1 2 3 4 5

Reader questions can also be stimulated through picture previews. During guided reading, this can occur during the picture walk at the opening of the lesson or by marking a key photo in the text with a sticky note and asking group members to start on that page rather than the beginning of the book. As they focus on developing questions about the pictures, prior knowledge is naturally activated and questions evolve easily in conversation.

FIGURE 10.3 Before-reading questioning: In picture #1, students generated questions.

FIGURE 10.4 In picture #2, you can see how they prepare to extend their thinking to generate possible answers to their questions as well. From *Baboons* (Dominie Press).

Previewing the Text Through Questioning

Name _____ Book _____

Pages Previewed _____ Date _____

Previewing Questions
As I previewed the illustrations
my questions are   Possible answers could include

_____   _____

_____   _____

_____   _____

_____   _____

After-Reading Reflections
The questions I answered correctly during the preview were about _____

_____

_____

I was able to answer them before reading because _____

_____

_____

During reading I discovered answers to _____

_____

_____

_____

_____

Guided Questioning: Cause and Effect Relationships

Cause and effect relationships are often essential to understanding concepts in science and social studies. To focus students on these important relationships, guided questioning sessions such as the following can be helpful. As discussed earlier, emergent students may engage in these questioning strategies orally while the teacher records their ideas while more proficient readers might write individually or in teams.

Science Example #1

Experiment: Placing blue food coloring into clear water and then adding a flower to the container.

WHAT HAPPENED?	WHY DID IT HAPPEN?
The water turned blue after the food coloring drops were added.	The food coloring mixed evenly throughout the water.
The flower turned blue.	The flower sucked the blue water up its stem and into the blossom.

Science Example #2

Reading a text about poisonous snakes, followed by a discussion of cause and effect, resulted in the following:

WHAT HAPPENED?	WHY DID IT HAPPEN?
The snake shed its skin.	It grew bigger and the skin was too tight.
The snake retreated from the approaching human.	The snake wasn't threatened by the human.
The snake coiled and struck at a mouse.	The mouse was food.

Social Studies Example #1

Topic: Why did this town turn into a ghost town?

WHAT HAPPENED?	WHY DID IT HAPPEN?
The people moved out of the town.	The mill closed down and there wasn't any work.

Social Studies Example #2

Topic: The pizza parlor went out of business.

WHAT HAPPENED?	WHY DID IT HAPPEN?
The pizza parlor closed.	People didn't like their pizza.
	Rent was raised and they couldn't afford it.

Understanding Cause and Effect Relationships in Informational Texts

Name _____ Book _____ Date _____

What happened?   Why did it happen?

_____   _____

_____   _____

_____   _____

_____   _____

_____   _____

_____   _____

As I think about cause and effect relationships in this text, I learned that

_____

_____

_____

_____

_____

_____

Conducting Interviews

Interviews are powerful stimulants to questioning. Students must give careful thought to questions for an interview as their purpose is authentic and a real human will respond. Interviews also help students to understand that different kinds of questions will elicit different kinds of responses.

As in any other kind of strategic teaching, it is important to model high-quality interview questions by first conducting a few class interviews and then discussing which kinds of questions got the most interesting answers. Which questions were not as helpful? These interviews might be of the principal, the secretary, cook, custodian, a student in the class, or a parent.

It is also important to provide opportunities for students of all ages to do primary source research by conducting interviews in which they take a larger share of the responsibility. The students conduct one-on-one interviews or work in teams to interview another person.

For these interviews, questions need to be prepared in advance and discussed before the actual interviews begin. With students of all ages, I encourage them to tape record the interview so they do not feel encumbered by trying to take notes during the interview. I find that this helps them to really listen to the answers provided during the interview and to more carefully consider the quality of the questions they had generated. The tape-recorded interview is helpful for reviewing the content at a later time.

As students gain proficiency with questioning in an interview format, I find they deepen their reflective thinking if they also consider questions such as the following that they might ask of an author, a character from history, or a scientist.

If you could interview a character from history such as Ben Franklin or Abe Lincoln, what would you ask?

If you could interview the author of this book about *space*, what would you want to know?

Preparing Interview Questions

Name _____ I will be interviewing _____

on the topic of _____ Date _____

		My rating for this question				
Question 1	Response	1	2	3	4	5
Question 2	Response	1	2	3	4	5
Question 3	Response	1	2	3	4	5
Question 4	Response	1	2	3	4	5

Postinterview Reflections:

The questions that worked especially well are _____

_____

As I think about the interview and my questions in general, I realize that

_____

_____

_____

If I were to conduct that same interview again, I would change my questions in the following ways:

_____

_____

_____

Teacher Observation

Student _____ Date _____

This student asks questions that	Yes	No
• Show self-monitoring of comprehension		
• Attempt to clarify confusion on the topic		
• Reach for more knowledge on the topic		
• Show application of prior knowledge		
• Reflect connections		
• Demonstrate understanding of main idea		
• Question the author's choices		
of words		
of organization		
of visual supports to the text		
topic clarity		
• Show critical thinking/evaluation		
• Wonder about the accuracy of information		
• Suggest integration of new information into understanding of the topic		
• Reflect on the learning		
• Extend beyond the text		

Questioning the Author

Questioning the Author was originally developed by Isabel Beck and Margaret McKeown, along with a group of colleagues at the University of Pittsburgh. It is a strategy that combines independent reading with guiding questions that students and teachers collaboratively ask of the text. The objective is to read the text section by section, ask questions similar to those listed below, and then discuss possibilities. It is important to follow each segment of reading with discussion and questioning. This ensures deeper levels of understanding.

SAMPLE QUESTIONS THAT MAY ASSIST STUDENTS
IN QUESTIONING THE AUTHOR

What is the author trying to say?

What is the author's message?

The author said _____, but what does it mean?

I can connect _____ in the text to _____ (something I read, experienced, or _____).

How does this information connect with earlier passages in the text?

Did the author explain this clearly? What's missing?

Is there anything we need to research to help us understand this?

Did the author give us an answer to _____?

(These questions have been modified from the original model.)

Beat the Teacher

In this strategy, students work in small groups to read short passages, stopping often to generate questions about the text. Their job is to read carefully and then generate questions on the topic *that the teacher has to answer!*

While the students are reading and writing their questions, the teacher also reads the passages, stopping often to write his or her own questions about the text.

When the time allocated for reading and question development has elapsed, the teacher takes a seat at the front of the room and students begin to ask questions about the text.

Their goal is to ask a question the teacher *can't* answer about the assigned reading. The students love this and are highly motivated to read carefully. Have fun!

Modifications

- Every time the teacher answers a question correctly, the students have to try to answer a teacher question.
- Give points for correct answers with the class and the teacher competing against each other.

Daily McGowan tried *Beat the Teacher* and was so pleased with the results that she wrote the following email:

Beat the Teacher

Daily McGowan

Dear Linda,

After hearing you talk about *Beat the Teacher* in a seminar, I decided to try it with the students I work with in Title I groups. It was so much fun! The children learned a lot. I didn't have to worry IF they were reading. They were highly motivated to ask tough questions. They read and re-read, then talked together to create really great questions. I tried it with students in first, third, and fifth grades and had wonderful success across the board. This strategy will become part of my permanent favorites! It was special because it was fun, motivating, and resulted in much more powerful learning than any questions I could ever generate.

11

Love Those Visuals
Photographs, Diagrams, and
Learning to Love Captions

Page layout in informational text serves a special comprehension function in that the various visual features exist to help readers link information-bearing sources together. For example, a caption's proximity to a photograph makes it clear that the caption is giving information about the photograph—the two elements go together (Donovan and Smolkin 2002).

Similarly, the size of a photograph makes a statement about its importance to the information. A large photograph says, "I am important. Look at me closely and search for details." The overall design of a page, the way the visuals and text work together, have a significant impact on the aesthetics of reading. Does this layout draw the reader into the topic, creating interest and wonder?

FIGURE 11.1 Notice how the proximity of the caption and the photo helps you realize that they work together. Notice also the mosquito photo on the lower left is larger than the flea. The discussion of the mosquito is the most important part of this two-page layout and the size of the photograph warns the reader. Notice also the visual appeal of this page—the small segments of text supported by photographs, a labeled diagram, and boldface text. From *What's Living at Your Place?* (Pacific Learning).

2. Itchy Biters

Do you sometimes get itchy bites? These may be caused by mosquitoes or fleas – two very small insects that often come into our homes.

Adult flea on cat fur

Adult mosquito

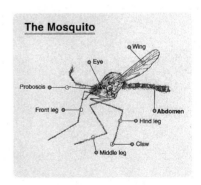

The Mosquito

Mosquitoes are small, two-winged flies. They are very common in **tropical** countries. Female mosquitoes need to **feed** on blood to produce eggs. They jab your skin with their sharp **proboscis** to suck up some blood. It's the **saliva** in their bite that makes your skin itchy.

11

FIGURE 11.2 Notice how the layout for this text includes text boxes and titles that have been framed to stand out, a flow chart, and interesting transitions between light and dark spaces. From *Kids Care for the Earth* (National Geographic for Kids).

Illustrations

Photographs, Drawings, Diagrams, Flow Charts, Sketches, Close-ups

In informational text, the illustrations deserve particular attention as they contain so much information. With the most emergent learners, the support of photographs and illustrations are critical to their ability to make meaning with limited amounts of print. The research on the relationship between illustrations and text suggests that pictures that illustrate statements made in the text enhance comprehension, while pictures that have only surface-level connections to the text, do not (Donovan and Smolkin 2002). So, if a text such as: "The mother cow feeds her baby" is accompa-

A spider can have
a hairy body.

FIGURE 11.3 Notice how the photograph clearly shows the hairy body of the spider that is described in the text. From *Spiders* (Newbridge).

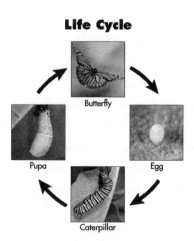

FIGURE 11.4 Notice the clear labeling of each part of the life cycle and the use of arrows to draw the eye through the stages of the life cycle. From *Fly Butterfly* (Newbridge).

nied by a photograph of a suckling calf, it is highly supportive of comprehension. A page with the same text and a general picture of cows and calves standing in a group has far less impact on understanding.

Similarly, a cross-section photograph or illustration that shows the roots of a plant reaching feelers out into the soil brings power to a text written about how plants get nutrients from the soil.

Water Wars

Rainwater soaks the soil around forest plants' roots. Tiny root hairs at the tips of the roots suck up the water and bits of minerals from the soil. Tiny tubes carry the water and minerals up the roots, up the stems, out the branches, and into every leaf. As they drink this "soup," plants get the minerals as well as the water they need to survive.

Sometimes water washes away the soil, and you can see the roots below a living plant.

FIGURE 11.5 The strong visuals in this text make the information come alive.

When we heighten reader awareness of these visuals, the way they are arranged on the page and the support they offer to meaning, we bring the visual into focus as tools for learning. It is unfortunate that many students, especially those most challenged as readers, have a tendency to pick up and immediately start reading, ignoring the very visuals that are there to make the reading easier.

Photographs that are generally related to the text but do not provide a visual interpretation of the text are less supportive of comprehension.

Analyzing Visuals: A Checklist

Analysis completed by   ❑ teacher   ❑ student

Text _____   Date _____

Photographs
❑ The photographs SHOW what the text describes.
❑ The photographs are detailed and of high quality.
❑ Photographs are of varying sizes to show that some ideas are more important than others.
❑ Could a student spend time looking at the picture(s) and learning?

What is the relationship of the visuals to the text?
❑ As you look at the two-page layout, are the readers' eyes guided through the pages?
❑ Is it clear where to start?
❑ Is it inviting?
❑ Can you tell which pictures support which portions of the text?
❑ Do the pictures support key concepts? (*Example:* The life cycle of a frog should be represented by photographs or drawings of each phase of development.)
❑ Do the illustrations add information, providing additional details beyond what is stated in the text?

Captions
❑ Are there captions with all or most pictures?
❑ Does the text of the caption directly relate to the photograph?
❑ Do the captions explain and expand understanding?
❑ Are there captions with diagrams, charts, and nonphotographic illustrations?

Other visuals
Does the book include:

❑ charts   ❑ maps
❑ graphs   ❑ timelines
❑ cross-section drawings   ❑ table of contents
❑ flow charts   ❑ glossary
❑ diagrams   ❑ index

Investigating Visual Supports

Review Team _____

Your job is to review at least ten informational books and think carefully about the visuals in the books. How do the visuals help you? Are these examples well chosen? Do the pages look inviting? Do they draw you into the reading? Why? Check for captions and other features we know support reading.

Book Reviewed   **Rating of the Visuals**

1. _____   5   4   3   2   1

Why did you give it this rating? _____

2. _____   5   4   3   2   1

Why did you give it this rating? _____

3. _____   5   4   3   2   1

Why did you give it this rating? _____

4. _____   5   4   3   2   1

Why did you give it this rating? _____

5. _____   5   4   3   2   1

Why did you give it this rating? _____

What did you learn about visuals and your own preferences?

_____

_____

_____

Exposing Students to a Wide Range of Visuals

As I broaden readers' understandings of the visuals that support their informational reading, I make a list of the visual formats I have introduced during read alouds, shared text experiences, and content area studies. Then, I carefully tally the number of times I provide minilessons on each format. My goal is to utilize this variety of visual formats across the curriculum and to support students in integrating these various visuals into their own writing of informational texts. I want students to consider visual features such as the number of visuals on a page, the impact of columns versus text that moves smoothly from left to right, and the visual role of titles and headings.

Sketching

There are times when a quick sketch is the perfect way to illustrate and support a point. To ensure that students understand the role sketching can play in their reading and their writing, I approach it in several ways.

While reading passages during an informational read aloud or a shared text experience, I stop frequently to think out loud about information I have just gleaned, then make a quick sketch on the chart showing what I have learned. I make stick figures, draw arrows, and add labels. I work in one color to make it clear that a sketch is different from an illustration. The way my sketches collect on a page is dependent upon the organization of the text I am reading.

If the text is linear, showing passage of time, I might draw arrows and have my sketches run horizontally. This works well for a biography, a historical recount, or a description of a life cycle.

If the text shows a cycle such as evaporation and precipitation, then my drawings are more likely to form a circle connected by arrows.

If the text is about an animal and has sections about habitat, eating habits, family groupings, and interesting facts I might group my sketches into a graphic organizer such as a web.

When I sketch to show what I am learning, I solidify my own understandings. It also gives the children a chance to hear the information one more time while I talk about it and then draw my sketch. I also support their learning by giving them another way to access and interpret the information as they look at my sketch.

FIGURE 11.6 Sketches solidify learning.

FIGURE 11.7 Both the teacher and student benefit from sketches. From the grade 1 classroom of Ali Taylor, McMinnville, Oregon.

Sketching My Way Through a Text

Reader _____ Topic: _____

1	**2**
3	**4**
5	**6**

How did sketching help you as a reader? Do you think you learned more? Why? Please prepare to share two of your sketches with a partner.

Using Visuals in Writing

As we support students in creating more powerful illustrations to accompany their informational writing, it can be helpful to remind them of the role their illustrations can play in conveying meaning. With guidance, students can learn how to create visuals that inform and support their messages.

Creating Visuals

Name of Writer _____   Topic _____

My most important ideas on this topic are:	I will explain this in		
	my writing (√)	my visuals (√)	both (√)
• _____			
• _____			
• _____			
• _____			
• _____			
• _____			
• _____			
• _____			
• _____			

Planning My Drawing

Writer _____ Topic _____ Date _____

I want my drawing to help me explain that _____

_____

continues

Planning My Drawing (*continued*)

The caption for my picture will say:

_____

```
┌─────────────────────────────────────────┐
│                                           │
│                                           │
│                                           │
│                                           │
└─────────────────────────────────────────┘
```

_____

My text will say:

```
┌─────────────────────────────────────────┐
│                                           │
│   _____    │
│                                           │
│   _____    │
│                                           │
│   _____    │
│                                           │
│   _____    │
│                                           │
│   _____    │
│                                           │
│   _____    │
│                                           │
│   _____    │
│                                           │
│   _____    │
│                                           │
└─────────────────────────────────────────┘
```

Planning a Visual to Teach and Inform

Writer _____ Topic _____ Date _____

As I plan my writing on this topic, the following visuals will best support the important ideas:

Most important ideas:	(✔) This will be supported by a											
	graph	diagram	flow chart	caption	cross-section drawing	sketch	illustration	photograph	time line	labels	a table	other____
_____												
_____												
_____												
_____												
_____												
_____												
_____												
_____												
_____												

Planning Multiple Illustrations on a Page

Student _____ Topic _____

Designers of informational texts often use several illustrations on a page and fit their text around the pictures, diagrams, and so on. Please plan a page that will support your topic. It needs to have at least three visuals (photograph, illustration, sketch, cross-section drawing, graph, diagram, or flow chart) and they should be of varying sizes. Make sure that the visual that is most important to your message is the largest. Your plan needs to include spaces for the text and captions as well. You may want to come up with more than one design and talk with a partner about which would be most interesting to look at.

Action Research on Visuals

In a recent seminar, I described an informal study I had conducted on how students use visuals. In this study some graduate students and I showed students a textbook page with diagrams, boldface words, labels, a title, headings, and captions for illustrations and then asked them how they might approach such a page.

Sharlene Goodwin, fifth-grade teacher and her student-teacher, Dick Kendrick, decided to replicate the study with their students. They work at Jefferson Elementary in Medford, Oregon.

Surveying Students

Sharlene Goodwin and Dick Kendrick

Dear Linda:

My student-teacher and I replicated the study you told about with the fifth graders in my building. We started with a survey asking students how they would approach informational texts.

We followed it with observations of students actually working with two different articles and compared the survey results, what the students said they did, with our observations.

The passage we chose was from a fifth-grade *Scholastic News* article entitled, "Olympic Torch Trail." The article included a map of the United States labeling states and the relay route for the 2002 Olympic torch drawn on the map. There were three pictures with captions either under or above the picture. There was large bold-faced print for titles and subheadings. The article was one page long. We created a list of my students rated by reading ability and divided them into below grade-level, at grade-level (average), and above grade-level readers. The following questions show the percentages answered by each group.

I have twenty-seven students in my class. Nine students are below average readers with two IEP students included in that group. Eight students are grade-level readers with two IEP students in that group. Seven students are above grade-level readers with one student in that group on a 504 plan.

The results of this survey gave us an idea of how this particular group of fifth-grade students reads an expository passage that includes labeled diagrams, pictures with captions, and titles and subheadings in boldfaced print. We used this information in planning instructional reading strategies to be taught during our current reading unit. We will post-test at the end of the unit to see if students are using visuals and boldfaced headings in an expository piece to a greater extent than they did at the beginning of the unit.

The outcome made me realize that we need to focus our reading instruction on making use of the visuals that accompany expository reading, including information in the margins, labeled diagrams, pictures, captions, and boldfaced or colored print. This may be a skill that good readers already use, but many below grade-level and average readers are missing.

QUESTIONS

1. When you first looked at page 6, did you begin reading the text first, or did you look at diagrams or illustrations first?

   Below—61% illustrations first

   Average—75% illustrations first

   Above—71% illustrations first

2. What picture or illustrations or diagram caught your attention first?

   Below—67% map, 33% pictures

   Average—63% map

   Above—71% map

3. Did you look back at the pictures when you were reading?

   Below—56% yes

   Average—75% yes

   Above—71% yes

4. Did the pictures help you to understand the article?

   Below—78% yes

   Average—50% yes

   Above—86% yes

5. Were the pictures or diagrams easy for you to understand?

   Below—78% yes

   Average—100% yes

   Above—100% yes

6. Did you look back at the pictures as you answered the questions?

   Below—89% yes

   Average—75% yes

   Above—88% yes

7. When you read normally, do you look at the illustrations first or do you start reading the text (words) first?

   Below—22% illustrations first

   Average—50% illustrations first

   Above—38% illustrations first

Some of the comments that were made about how the illustrations helped:

Below—They told me things I did not learn in the story. It showed me how many states the torch passed through.

Average—I know now that stars and ordinary people can both hold the torch.
They helped by telling me where they were.

Above—It helped by showing where the relay started and where it went.
I saw the people the article was talking about.

As we worked with additional articles, we observed the different responses received as students interacted with different visuals. One article used a large map of the United States to plot the route of the Olympic Torch. The size of this graphic attracted their attention more than the other visuals on the page. This map was the main visual on the page and the use of it was very important to understand the content of the article. The second article contained several small pictures with one larger picture of the Pentagon centered at the top of the page. There was a small map showing where the Pentagon, Trade Center buildings, and the plane crash were located. Students didn't seem to use the visuals on the second article as much as they did on the first article.

Comparing answers from articles one and two to answers from the survey show that students don't always put into practice the strategies they have learned and know they should use. It is evident that we need to spend more time practicing this strategy with our group of students.

We gave our two ESL students the survey today, but because they are in a pull-out program they missed some of the reading sessions. One speaks fluent English but is a low-ability reader. He said he looks at pictures first before reading text and that illustrations are helpful to him. The other speaks only broken English, is an above grade-level reader in Spanish, but below grade-level reader in English. He said that he looks at illustrations first if the article is in English, and he reads the text first if it is in Spanish. Both agreed that visuals on a page were important. We hope you find this information useful.

Cheryle Ferlita is an educator from Tampa, Florida who has taught in a variety of settings including elementary and secondary education as well as special education. She is currently serving as a district-level staff developer. Cheryl loves to work with informational texts. Her enthusiasm shows in her work with students and in the following reflection on visual presentations.

Visual Presentations

Cheryle Ferlita

Developing Visual Presentations

I teach and model several ways to visually represent an understanding of nonfiction text. After modeling, I allow students to independently select a format that best represents the information in a text of their choosing. Here are some examples of possible guided reading lessons and student responses.

PROCEDURE:

1. Select a text with visual supports such as charts, maps, graphs, diagrams, photos, illustrations, captions, and/or table of contents.
2. Have students read a selected section of the text. Discuss how they would want to visually represent the text and why. Use guided questioning and discussion to help them to see that there may be more than one appropriate way to represent the information.
3. Model and/or have students discuss what visual might best represent the information. Guide them through this discussion prompting as needed. This discussion will enhance their comprehension of the text.
4. Have students read another selected part of the text. Allow time for them to work in cooperative groups to develop a visual presentation of the text.
5. Have students share their formats discussing the key points of the text.
6. Move toward independent presentations throughout the text or another text.
7. Have students self-evaluate their presentations.

FIGURE 11.8
Three students read *How Plants Survive* by Kathleen Kudlinski (Newbridge) and created the visual representations shown in Figures 11.9, 11.10, and 11.11.

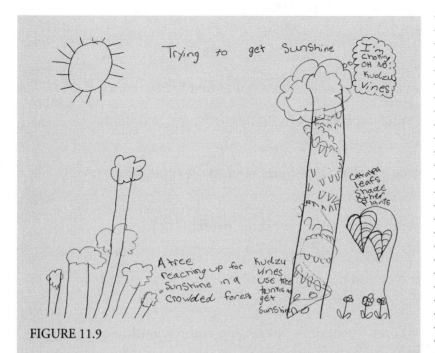

FIGURE 11.9

Plant	How they compete for sunshine
kudzu vine	races up a tree trunk toward the sun
Sugar maple	grows tall in a crowded forest grows wide in an open sunny field
Catalpa leaf	shades other plants and has a big leaf to get sun
Pine tree needles	thousands of needles they soak up sunshine

FIGURE 11.10

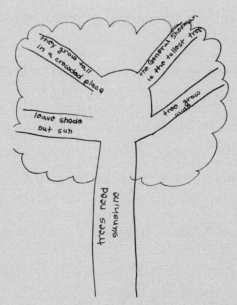

FIGURE 11.11 These visual representations of *How Plants Survive* show three unique yet thorough efforts to reflect and personalize their learning.

Student Self-Evaluation for Visual Representation

❏ I have selected a format that matches the type of text I read.

❏ I have included the most important information from the text in my visual presentation.

❏ I have put the necessary information from all of the text into the presentation.

❏ I can tell others or write about what my visual presentation represents.

❏ I have done my best work on my visual presentation. I have edited and revised for completeness and organization.

❏ I have made my visual representation interesting and relevant to the topic.

Teacher Evaluation for Visual Representations

❏ The student can independently select a format that is appropriate for the text type.

❏ The student can determine the most important information from the text and what information is not relevant to the presentation.

❏ The student is able to synthesize the information in the text into one whole piece of visual information.

❏ The student can provide oral and written support for the visual presentation.

❏ The student develops a visual presentation that is neat and organized.

❏ The student can examine other visual presentations and evaluate their appropriateness.

12

Text Features
It Isn't Just the Words

Informational text has many features that are designed to support readers in navigating through resources and providing reader-friendly access to content. When readers expect these features and know how to use them, they can move in and out of informational texts, selecting pages that will provide the most assistance on their topic, connecting pictures and text blocks, and accessing information with efficiency and comprehension.

Reflections such as these can serve to heighten awareness of text features:

How many features did you find?

Which book had the most features?

What was the affect on you as a reader when a book was missing features?

Exploring Captions

Review captions in a variety of books. Try to find examples of captions that summarize, elaborate, add information beyond the text, describe visuals, connect to a chart or diagram, or explain a chart. Find a Big Book or resource book that needs captions. You can choose a book that doesn't have any or one that needs more. Use sticky notes to add captions to the illustrations and then share your captions with a friend.

Making the Most of Diagrams

Diagrams are important visual supports that often carry more information than the text itself. When students take time to look at diagrams before reading or to draw a diagram to support their writing, they are engaging in multiple systems of communication that assist in long-term memory.

Note the different perspectives and formats in the following diagrams:

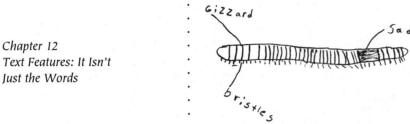

FIGURE 12.1 A full-view diagram often is accompanied by labels and an attempt at detail.

FIGURE 12.2

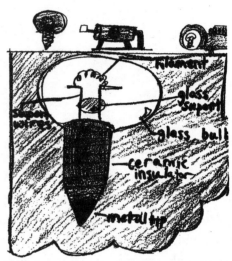

FIGURE 12.3

A close-up diagram is a drawing or photograph as though seen from the perspective of a magnifying glass or a microscope. The idea is to look at a part of the whole, very closely.

FIGURE 12.4

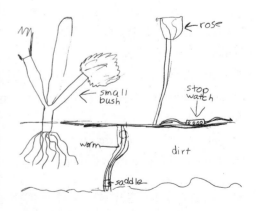

FIGURE 12.5

Cutaway diagrams such as the two shown here are like a slice of the real thing. They might show the inside of a piece of fruit, the inside of an animal, or the interior and underground workings of a plant.

Making the Most of a Table of Contents

The table of contents may be one of the most useful features in informational texts. Once children catch on to the benefits, they use them eagerly and happily volunteer to create tables of contents for books that have sadly forgotten to include one. I love the energy that flows when they realize a book doesn't have a table of contents. There is usually a high-energy conversation over, "What ARE the sections in this book? We need to have headings for chapters to be able to make a contents page. What should the headings be?" and so on. Even the most emergent readers quickly learn the joys of writing their own table of contents. Small sticky notes are great for adding headings to pages and large sticky notes, placed inside of the front cover, work well for the insertion of a student-created table of contents.

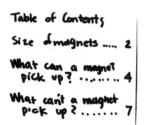

A magnet can pick up paper clips.

But a magnet can't pick up any of these things.

FIGURE 12.6

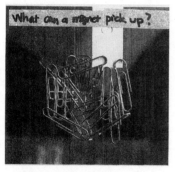

FIGURE 12.7

Table of contents predictions. In Figure 12.6, first graders used sticky notes to add headings to pages 4 and 7 and then, in Figure 12.7, created a table of contents for this book. The same process works well in Big Books.

FIGURE 12.8 Students can use the table of contents to predict content and words that are likely to occur in each chapter, then read to find out how their ideas matched those of the author.

Table of Contents Predictions

Chapter # _____ Title _____

Topics I predict

_____

_____

_____

_____

_____

_____

Words I predict

_____

_____

_____

_____

_____

_____

Understanding Graphs

Math Their Way taught us many years ago to engage primary students in making graphs about real things in their lives. This supported mathematical concepts and demonstrated clearly how graphs are used. Children enjoy and learn from a wide range of the following activities:

Graph the number of people who wear shoes with buckles, ties, and slip-ons

Graph the foods we ate for breakfast. Who ate:

cereal, eggs, fruit, toast, milk, juice, pancakes, did not eat

Make a circle graph to show which percentage of students ride the bus

Make a circle graph to show the percentage of those eating hot lunch today

The languages spoken in our families

Explore graphs in text and discuss why a graph is helpful. Why would an author choose a graph instead of just writing about the topic?

Charts

What do they do? How do they help us?

_____

_____

FIGURE 12.9 The chart is the focus of this page from _National Geographic for Kids_.

What can you learn from the chart? Why did the author choose a chart? What are the advantages and disadvantages? When you read the text, is the information from the chart repeated, explained in a different way, or not addressed? Why?

_____

_____

If you had written this article, would you have chosen a chart or some other format?

_____

_____

Examine your writing folder. Are there any places where a chart would support your writing?

_____

_____

Flow Charts Show Steps in a Process

Make a flow chart showing what you have learned about a life cycle. It could be the life cycle of a butterfly, a frog, a human, or a plant. Illustrate each stage and include a caption to explain.

Flow Chart for the Life Cycle of _____ Created by _____

(caption)   (caption)

(caption)   (caption)

Making Informational Text Features

A book of informational text features can be a very helpful resource when formatted as a Big Book or small versions created by individuals.

Within a unit of study, work with the students to construct a resource that has one page dedicated to each informational text feature.

For example:

A Book About Whales

"In this book we show what we learned about whales and created a resource we can use all year to remind ourselves of the important features we can use in informational reading and writing."

EXAMPLE:

Text feature highlighted

Page one.   Whales   Table of Contents
Page two.   The Body of the Whale   Diagram
Page three.   Migration   Boldface type
Page four.   Whale Babies   Caption
Page five.   Whales are Intelligent   Cross-section diagram with labels
Page six.   Kinds of Whales   Chart with length, weight
Page seven.   Index

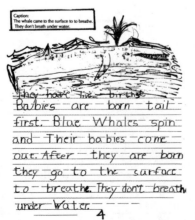

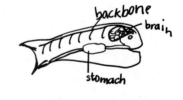

FIGURE 12.10 Illustrations for features book.

Pam Tate, reading specialist in McMinnville, Oregon, helps students to notice and understand a table of contents by having them analyze a published book and then creating a student-authored table of contents for the book:

Making Your Own Table of Contents

Pam Tate

Our second-grade guided reading group read several nonfiction books, looking at the format of each. We looked at how the table of contents, indexes, subtitles, and captions helped us better understand the text.

When we started reading a book about how animals move, the students noticed that there was no table of contents. It was suggested that we make one using sticky notes to help other readers understand the book better.

We revisited some of the other books we had read, looking at the contents page and discussing how the author had decided what to put on that page. We then went back to our book and used sticky notes to mark the different parts of the book. We talked about the most important ideas and what would really help the reader know what the book was about.

The students debated if the table of contents should list the names of the different animals or list the different ways that animals move. They finally came to a consensus that it would be better to put down the word that told how the animal moved, e.g., *flying, running,* and so on, as they felt that was the main idea of the book.

Sticky notes were handed out and students went to work. There were some variations so when everyone was finished, they tried each other's table of contents to see how they worked! With lots of modeling and investigating of texts, plus making our own contents page, the students now have a keen awareness of the table of contents and how it works.

Part Three
Small Group Experiences with Informational Texts

Having time to read books and materials of your own choosing is absolutely necessary to becoming a reader. Recreational reading promotes comprehension, vocabulary, conventional spellings, grammar, writing competency, and a positive attitude toward the written word.

Regie Routman

13

Guided Reading with Informational Texts

It has been well established that guided reading supports readers in developing independent strategies with text. As informational texts are integrated into guided reading sequences, reading skills are taught along with content-seeking skills. This unifies the curriculum and supports learners in understanding that they can transfer their learning across all curricular areas.

Lesson Design

The lesson design for informational guided reading is much like that of a fiction lesson, except that there is a stronger emphasis on activating and building prior knowledge to ensure that the content-specific vocabulary and concepts are ready to apply to the reading. In addition, informational guided reading requires that the reader understand the role of textual features such as captions and visuals, as well as organizational features such as a table of contents or index.

Sample Lesson Design

Warm up: Emergent readers re-read familiar favorites.

Fluent readers may use this as time to preview the text or refresh their thinking from previous reading on the topic

Introducing the Text

Take time to talk about experiences that relate to the topic and any connections that can be made. If possible, engage in a real experience related to the topic. Ensure that concepts and vocabulary are well integrated into the prereading discussion and that time is taken to discuss the layout of the informational text, supportive text features, and the purpose for reading. Students may benefit from asking personal questions on the topic to establish a purpose for reading. This is also a time when a comprehension strategy could be demonstrated and encouraged.

Independent Reading of the Text

Students read independently while the teacher circulates and listens to individuals. They may read a paragraph, a page, or several pages depending upon the teaching point and the fluency level of the readers. Periodically bring the students back together to discuss, set new purposes, and consider the content being learned. Provide for fast finishers with directions such as: "If you finish reading these two pages before I give the signal for talk, please use the time to review the reading and prepare for a retell." Or, "Please use the time to skim for important words."

Discussing the Text

Discuss the content. What did we learn? Discuss informational reading strategies. What strategies helped us as readers? Did we use the captions and headings; the pictures; the table of contents? What goals could we set for ourselves as informational text readers?

Literacy Skills to Support in Guided Reading of Informational Texts

Comprehension

Recall

Retell

Predicting and verifying predictions

Compare/contrast

Cause/effect

Main idea

Supporting details

Making connections

   Text to self

   Text to world

   Text to text

Visualizing

Draw conclusions

Locating information, in a text, on a page, within a paragraph

Finding key words, ideas

SELF-MONITORING FOR UNDERSTANDING

Classifying

Self-questioning

Making inferences

Critical analysis: making judgments, seeing multiple perspectives, checking sources

COMPREHENSION AT THE WORD LEVEL

Dealing with challenging words

Using context to determine word meaning

Developing technical vocabulary

Using letters, sounds, chunks of words

Using fix-up strategies

Using the glossary

Using a thesaurus

Using a dictionary

TEXT FEATURES

Illustrations, looking for details	Table of contents
Labels	Glossary
Captions	Index
Boldface type	Diagrams
Headings	Maps
Questions as headings	Charts
Picture glossary	Summary charts

ORGANIZATIONAL FEATURES

Text structures (directions, cause/effect, time/order, description, problem/solution, comparison/contrast)

Using lists

Following steps in directions

Question-answer format

Finding topic sentences, directions

Informational Book Sorts

A guided reading lesson doesn't always need to be about one book. Sometimes a guided reading lesson can utilize many books with a goal of understanding text features. To engage in this kind of guided reading lesson, I gather a wide array of informational books that represent familiar favorites, as well as books on topics that are of interest to the students.

We then begin to sort the titles according to the teaching point I have selected. If the group needs support in understanding text features, we might sort according to books with a table of contents, books with captions, books with an index, books with labels on drawings, and so on. The students can discuss the features they locate and compare across books. How is the index in book #1 like the index in #2. . . . What are the common features of tables of contents? What do we notice about diagrams?

Book sorts could be conducted for books that show passage of time, books that compare and contrast, books that show cause and effect, books that describe, books that tell how to, and so on.

Searching for Informational Text Features

Our guided reading group has read the following books and we found:

Book	Table of Contents	Index	Glossary	Boldface	Captions	Titles	Diagrams	Labels on Drawings

Text Feature Scavenger Hunt

Reader _____ Date _____

Your job is to investigate text features and try to find examples of as many different features as you can. Be sure to list the feature, its purpose and the text in which you found it.

TEXT FEATURE	PURPOSE	FOUND IN	PAGE
_____	_____	_____	_____
_____	_____	_____	_____
_____	_____	_____	_____
_____	_____	_____	_____
_____	_____	_____	_____
_____	_____	_____	_____
_____	_____	_____	_____
_____	_____	_____	_____
_____	_____	_____	_____
_____	_____	_____	_____
_____	_____	_____	_____
_____	_____	_____	_____

Using the Table of Contents

Reader _____ Book _____

Before reading: Look at the table of contents.

Select a chapter you think would answer a question you have on the topic.

_____

Predict four content words you think could appear in that chapter.

_____   _____   _____   _____

Write a question you hope will be answered in the chapter.

_____

_____

After reading the chapter:

Was your question answered? Why or why not?

_____

Were your words in the text? Were there any synonyms for your words?

_____

What were some other words that you thought were important?

_____

continues

Using the Table of Contents (*continued*)

Select another chapter and go again!

_____

_____

_____

How does the table of contents help you as a reader?

_____

_____

Did the chapter headings really reflect the content? Is there anything you
would change? Are the section titles interesting and descriptive? Could you
rewrite them to make them better?

_____

_____

_____

_____

_____

_____

_____

Using Boldface Type

Guide a group of readers through a text with boldface type such as the one below. Discuss why the author would make some words bold and not others and how you might determine the meaning of boldface words. What strategies might you use to find the meaning? Are there signal words to help you?

The Rainforest Canopy

The trees in a rainforest are very tall. The tallest trees are as high as a 20-story building. The top layer of trees is called the **canopy**. The leaves in the canopy get a lot of sun.

FIGURE 13.1 Notice how the definition for *canopy* actually appears before the word. The signal words: *is called . . .* are a clue students need to learn to notice. From *The Rain Forest* (Dominie, 2000).

Their Diet

Baboons are **omnivores**. This means they eat both plants and animals. They use their hands to eat and to dig up roots and bulbs. Grass is a large part of their diet. Baboons eat other plant foods including leaves, flowers, fruits and berries, seeds, shoots, twigs, bark, and mushrooms.

A baboon's diet also includes grasshoppers, spiders, lizards, frogs, fish, birds' eggs, and small mammals.

FIGURE 13.2 Notice how the definition for *omnivores* is not in the same sentence as the focus word. The signal words: *this means . . .* are a clue.

Finding the Topic Sentence

Topic sentences can be helpful to readers. In this guided reading lesson, I would ask students to read paragraphs with the goal of locating topic sentences in each one. Which sentence gives a main idea for the paragraph? Which sentences just provide details? Where is the topic sentence located? Is it at the beginning, middle, or end of the paragraph?

Topic Sentences

Reflection by _____ (reader)

Text read _____

In this book, I noticed that the topic sentences were easy to find ☐ or hard to find ☐. I think this was because

_____

The topic sentences appeared in the following portions of the paragraphs: (Tally the topic sentences according to the portion of the paragraph in which they appear.)

BEGINNING	MIDDLE	END
_____	_____	_____
_____	_____	_____
_____	_____	_____

My observations about topic sentences and how I might use them as a writer:

_____

_____

_____

_____

_____

_____

Guided Reading for Author Study

Lead a guided reading group in reading several works by an author such as Gail Gibbons, Seymour Simon, or Russell Freeman. Discuss attributes of their writing and what makes them successful writers of informational texts. Now, read the work of another informational author. What do you notice about the changes in style, visual layouts, and so on?

Noticing the Writers Craft as We Read

Title	Author	Observations of Craft
Storms	Seymour Simon	Analogy. . . . Hailstones like baseballs
		Supports visualizing with clear descriptions
		Powerful verbs: *smashes, pounds, spins*
Joyful Noise	Paul Fleischman	Facts written for two readers
		Personification: assigns human feelings to insects

What have you learned as a writer of informational text?

Guided Reading of Directions

Guide a group through two sets of directions such as recipes, directions for assembling a toy, or operating a computer. Compare and list the following: What do we notice about directions? What features need to be present? Are some directions more effective and easy to understand than others? Why?

Have the guided reading group follow one set of directions and then prepare to teach the class what they have learned.

The following recipe makes wonderful ice cream. It is a great science lesson as well as a guided reading experience.

Making Ice Cream

INGREDIENTS

Canned evaporated milk   Egg substitute

Fresh milk   Vanilla flavoring

Sugar

SUPPLIES NEEDED

Zip lock bags (1 gallon and   Ice

    1 quart sizes)   Rock salt

Measuring spoons   Gloves or mittens

Work with a partner to place the following ingredients in the small zip lock bag:

1 tablespoon evaporated milk

1 cup milk

2 tablespoons sugar

1 tablespoon egg substitute

1/8 teaspoon vanilla flavoring

Zip the bag. Remove as much air as possible.

Gently shake the bag to mix the ingredients.

Place the bag with the ice cream mix into the large zip lock bag. Put ice all around the smaller bag and
    sprinkle it with a handful of rock salt.

Put on gloves or mittens.

Work with your partner to gently keep the bag moving for ten minutes.

You are ready to eat the ice cream when it looks solid. Enjoy!

Make It Real by Linda Hoyt (Heinemann: Portsmouth, NH); © 2002

Let's Share!

During the independent reading portion of an informational guided
reading lesson, ask the students to begin thinking of what they would
include in a retell of the content. After reading, I then ask them to draw
and/or write the key points they want to make. They share with partners
with the goal of helping their partner to add information to the retell
they have organized. This may mean they borrow a bit from each other,
return to the text to search for more information, or turn to an
additional resource.

Reading Informational Texts

Reader _____ Date _____

As a reader of informational texts, I am learning that _____

_____

When I am getting ready to read I take time to _____

_____

During reading I know it is important to _____

_____

If I get stuck on a word, I_____

_____

Strategies I am using a lot in informational reading_____

_____

When I am finished reading I _____

_____

A goal for my next informational book is to _____

_____

Informational books are different from stories because _____

_____

_____

Guided Reading Self-Assessment (Primary)

❏ I used the pictures to think about each page.

When I had trouble with a word, I:

❏ Checked the picture

❏ Thought about what makes sense

❏ Used beginning sounds

❏ Used ending sounds

❏ Chunked the word

I did a retell of this book and included:

❏ Lots of important ideas

❏ A few important ideas

❏ Not so many ideas

When I read this book again, I am going to work on _____

_____

_____

_____

_____

_____

_____

_____

Book Evaluation

Name _____ Date _____

Name of Book _____ Author _____

	GREAT	OK	NOT SO GREAT
The author made the information easy to understand.	1 2	3 4	5 6
The writing style was comfortable to read.	1 2	3 4	5 6
The book was organized in a logical way.	1 2	3 4	5 6
The author explained ideas completely before shifting topics.	1 2	3 4	5 6
The charts, graphs, pictures, and other visuals were helpful.	1 2	3 4	5 6
The table of contents and index were organized and easy to use.	1 2	3 4	5 6
My overall rating of this book:	1 2	3 4	5 6

Notetaking Guide

Name _____ Date _____

Title of Book _____ Author _____

FACTS FROM THE TEXT	PG #	MY CONNECTIONS	MY QUESTIONS

_____

_____

_____

_____

_____

_____

I think the author's purpose was _____

_____

_____

My observations about the text structure, use of visuals, quality of descriptions, and so on: _____

_____

_____

_____

_____

Guided Reading with News Articles

While news magazines written expressly for students are wonderful tools for teaching reading strategies in informational texts, I like to ensure that strategies have come full circle by providing opportunities for students to interact with real newspapers as well. Newspapers provide authentic opportunities to interact with current events and local news and issues, and to promote reading on topics of personal interest.

As I guide students through newspaper reading during guided reading, I want to support navigational strategies such as skimming, scanning, using photographs and titles, and shifting reading to columns rather than a left-to-right progression. I believe this is a critical opportunity to see if students shift strategies to match their shifting purposes. For example, if I was picking up a newspaper just to check out current events, my navigational strategy would probably bring me to the front page and the metro sections so that I could preview both local and national issues. If my purpose was to find out the scores from yesterday's game, I would go straight to the sports section. A hunt for a new computer printer might take me either to the business section or to the classified ads, and so on. When navigational strategies respond to purpose, we operate more efficiently in informational text. Readers who are really looking for the classified ads but shift aimlessly through piles of papers without using the index or remembering that classifieds have a different look to cue up our search, are readers who will be just as aimless doing research in a content area study.

FIGURE 13.3 Newspapers are powerful tools for guided reading.

I also want to ensure that students are utilizing a full range of good reader strategies while they read. As a result, I often provide post-it notes to encourage comprehension strategies such as notetaking, visualization, self-questioning, and connections. I can support critical literacy by having them read two articles on the same topic and discuss the way the information was communicated, point of view, or accuracy of information. Word-level knowledge could be supported through postreading word searches for adjectives, nouns, verbs, and two-, three-, and four-syllable words.

Explorations of the classified ads can also be powerful guided reading lessons as students consider the shifts in writing style from a news article or purposes for reading classified ads.

Primary students also benefit from interactions with the newspaper. I find that kindergarten and first-grade students pick up amazing amounts of information from studying the pictures, asking questions, and then interacting with the articles themselves.

Assessing Strategies with a Newspaper

Reader _____ Focus Newspaper _____

Date _____

The reader is able to:

❏ Shift navigational strategies to match a purpose for reading

❏ Recognize and utilize columns when reading

❏ Use photographs and captions

❏ Explain the shifts in language and style between articles, letters to the editor, classified ads, and advertisements

❏ Use tables and graphs such as in the sports and business sections

❏ Discuss point of view in an article

Searching Informational Texts

Great opening: I thought it was great because:

_____

_____

_____

_____

Great descriptions: I thought it was great because:

_____

_____

_____

_____

Great visuals: I thought it was great because:

_____

_____

_____

_____

Informational Reading Checklist

Name _____ Date _____

Text Read _____

❑ Takes time to preview text before reading

❑ Uses illustrations, boldface, and title to predict

❑ Generates personal questions about the reading

❑ Visualizes, including details

❑ Makes inferences about the text

❑ Finds justification for opinions within text

❑ Can summarize/retell main ideas and key points

❑ Integrates information from text and visuals

❑ Gains additional information from captions

❑ Uses index

❑ Uses table of contents

❑ Uses glossary

Informational Reading Strategy Reflections

Reader _____ Text _____ Date _____

At the text level, this student is remembering to . . .

	Most of the Time	Sometimes	Not Yet	Comments
Use picture clues to predict				
Use visuals to cross-check meaning				
Think about meaning				
Self-monitor comprehension				
Self-correct				
Integrate visual information with information from the text				
Read smoothly and with appropriate phrasing				

At the word level, this student is remembering to . . .

☐ Re-read to check and confirm

☐ Use context to determine word meaning

☐ Use beginning and ending sounds

☐ Chunk unknown words

Reading Strategy Observation

Name _____ Date _____ Text Read _____

During this observation, I saw evidence that this student was:

	Comments Evidence of Use	Most of the Time	Sometimes	Not Yet	Comments
Using prior knowledge					
Self-questioning					

Making connections:
   Text to self
   Text to world
   Text to text					

Visualizing					
Identifying important words and ideas					
Making inferences					
Drawing conclusions					
Summarizing					

Retelling Scoring Guide for Informational Text

6 The reader states all main ideas and provides supporting details. Key concepts are understood accurately and extensions may be offered in the form of opinions or connections.

4 The reader is able to state most of the main ideas and provides a range of supporting details. Most concepts are understood accurately.

2 The reader identifies some main ideas and a few supporting details. There may be a few inaccuracies or underdeveloped concepts.

1 The reader is not able to identify the main ideas. Information is incomplete and/or inaccurate.

Skimming and Scanning

Reader _____ Text _____ Date _____

As you use skimming and scanning in your reading today, think carefully about how the strategies influenced your reading.

Skim
You want to do this quickly and think . . .

- What kind of reading is this? What is the topic?

  _____

- What challenges might I be prepared for? Is this a topic which is new for me? Do I know something about it? Is the page layout unusual?

  _____

- What supports are here? Is there a table of contents, boldface words, headings or other support? Are there photographs, diagrams, or illustrations to help me?

  _____

Scan
Now you are using magnifying glass to look closely at the text . . . Take it a little slower and start getting into the topic.

- Read the title, the headings, and skim the biggest pictures. Wonder. What will this be about? What are the big ideas?

  _____

- Look at the table of contents. What topics will be addressed?

  _____

- Check out the index and glossary. Do some of these words look familiar?

  _____

Read
You are ready to read. Take your time. Think about your ideas from skimming and scanning. Are they matching what you are learning?

  _____

Reflect
How did skimming and scanning help you as a reader?

  _____

Once Isn't Enough!

First Time Around: Skim . . .

What do you notice?

What do you think the key points might be?

What words do you predict?

Second Time Around: Scan . . .

Read slowly . . . (bring out the magnifying glass!)

Identify key words and ideas.

Use sticky notes to mark key points.

TALK to a partner. Reach agreement on the important points.

Third Time Around: Synthesize/Summarize . . .

Quiz yourself.

Write questions that could be on a test. If you were writing a test, what would you ask?

Think and talk. Why is this information important?

Key Words

In this strategy, students learn to read fairly short segments of text, then identify a key word or phrase that summarizes that segment. They end up with a list of words that can be easily used to generate an oral or written summary. The words can be collected on sticky notes, on sheets of paper, or in a shared book experience, by the teacher.

FIGURE 13.4 This page from *What Is Rain?* (Dominie) is used for the key word strategy.

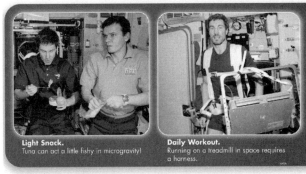

Using the page shown in Figure 13.5, students can identify numerous key words. Some of the words include:

Sleep

Standing up

Old—food in tubes

Now—plastic bags

Shower water flies

Could wreck computers

Waste water

Vacuumed out

Wall-to-Wall Sleeping
In microgravity there's no need for a bed. Astronauts can snooze while floating upside down in the middle of a room. But there's a chance they could "drift off" and bump against computer controls. So at night, they strap themselves into sleeping bags that hang from the walls.

"Sleeping in space is very relaxing," Shepherd says. "You're not weighed down by gravity, so you don't feel anything pressing on your skin."

No More Mushed Chicken
Supply ships bring meals to the station only once a month. That means astronaut food needs to stay fresh a long time.

Foods like chicken and peas used to be kept fresh by mushing them up and sealing them in tubes. At mealtime, astronauts would squirt out the food like toothpaste.

Luckily, scientists found new ways to kill the microbes that make food rot. Some space foods, such as scrambled eggs and fruit punch, are dried out. Astronauts just add water. Others, such as hot dogs and beef stew, are sealed in microbe-blocking plastic bags. Astronauts heat the bags before mealtime. Treats like candy and gum can stay fresh for a month without help.

"I thought the Russian food was a little tastier than the American food," Shepherd says. "They had good soups—chicken and rice was my favorite. But no one was very picky."

To keep their meals from floating away, astronauts often slot food packages into special trays, then strap the trays to their legs.

Bathroom Activities
In microgravity, water from a shower flies in all directions. Floating water droplets could damage ISS computers. So instead of taking showers, space station residents rub water and soap over their bodies, then sponge off.

In orbit, you can't rely on gravity to tug wastewater down the pipes of a toilet. The space model works like a vacuum cleaner, using a stream of air to pull waste into sealed containers. The containers are then sent off in spacecraft that land on Earth, or in smaller craft designed to burn up in Earth's atmosphere.

WebLink **ISS Tracker** Find out where the International Space Station is in the sky, and if you can see it from your home. Go to www.nationalgeographic.com/ngforkids/articles.

FIGURE 13.5 Key words can be used to generate oral or written summaries that are concise and to the point. From *Exploring Space* (National Geographic for Kids).

Very Important Points Strategy (VIP)

Have students cut sticky notes so that there are slim strips of paper extending out from the sticky edge, like fringe.

As they read, the goal is to place VIPs (Very Important Point markers) in the text to indicate the most important ideas. These points may be points of interest, points of confusion, or a place where the student remembered a connection.

At the end of reading, students meet in pairs or small groups and discuss the VIPs they selected. To take this to a higher level, you could even ask students to come to a consensus about the VIPs for a particular section, justifying their decisions with points in the text.

I find that it helps to give students a limited number of points they can mark in a section or a page. If they have unlimited numbers of points to mark, they mark too much and have difficulty distilling the key ideas.

Since I wrote about the VIP strategy in 1999 (*Revisit, Reflect, Retell*), I have heard from many teachers who have used the strategy. They tell me it is great because you don't have to go to the copy machine. It works in any book and students love the kinesthetic action of placing sticky note strips onto pages and then discussing their choices.

Amy Goodman, a middle school teacher in Anchorage, Alaska writes:

Using VIP with Middle School Students

Amy Goodman

I used your sticky note fringe lesson (VIP), and I wanted to let you know how effective it was with my eighth graders. I teach an elective class called "Strategies for Success." These 20 kids are all from my team. In essence, I am their "study hall" teacher. My science partner had assigned an article to read with a half-page summary, and a half-page response to be written. I watched as the kids made attempts and it was clear they had no idea how to approach the task. Luckily, I had just attended your workshops and was able to pull out a strategy to help them along.

I gave them all sticky notes and showed how to make the fringe. Because I limited their fringe pieces to three to four, they felt less overwhelmed with the task of identifying the main points on the first page of the article. I explained that they should use a sticky note piece of fringe when they felt that they read something important. I read aloud the article and stopped after the first paragraph. I did a think aloud showing the kids where I had placed my fringe. We continued with the reading and at the end of the page we traded ideas. It was interesting to see which learners picked out main ideas as they went and which learners waited until the end to make an evaluation of the content. Clearly, having both approaches used in the class allowed others to learn another way of approaching the same task.

I've used highlighters before with the kids, but the sticky note fringe gave them the opportunity to change their minds. This really boosted their confidence knowing it was easy to change their minds without leaving a messy trail. I also think they got quickly engaged because of the tactile approach—tearing the fringe and moving it around kept them busy. Reading the article as they evaluated the content helped them focus on finding the main points. I slowly moved them into reading the article on their own after they were fully engaged.

The kids moved quickly into writing summaries once they had all that information narrowed down to a few points on every page. The task didn't overwhelm them when they saw how easy it was to put those main ideas into sentences for their half-page summaries.

This was a very successful strategy and I know they "got it" because I have since seen kids using it on their own.

I also pulled out the sticky note fringe recently in my language arts class. We were reading Roald Dahl's story "The Landlady" in their literature text. Because I was going to focus on the skill of foreshadowing, I wanted the kids to highlight passages within the text that made them feel uneasy since this story is a bit on the dark side. Obviously, they couldn't use highlighters in their textbooks, so the sticky note fringe strategy came to the rescue. Again, my students felt great success. I think they especially enjoyed watching each other make judgments while reading the short story. They couldn't help but notice the variety of marked passages at their table groups. This led to a very productive lesson on the writer's craft of foreshadowing. Students found no difficulty in writing an expository paragraph about the use of foreshadowing in this story because the information had been narrowed down before they attempted to write.

I think teachers sometimes forget to model the step of how to gather the information before asking students to write. We forget that this is a learned skill that needs to be modeled and practiced.

Notemaking

Students often are asked to take notes on index cards. This works for some students but leaves others feeling puzzled and unsure.

I believe that even primary students need to learn to take notes. I start with a picture in an enlarged text or in a guided reading selection and ask the students to look very closely. What can they learn from just the picture? Then, I make a list of their ideas on chart paper or by placing sticky notes directly onto the picture. They soon get the idea and are ready to do it alone.

The next step is to work with notetaking from the text. Now, we read the text, talk about important ideas, and jot down our notes. The hardest part is limiting the notes to just a few words. (If you do the key word strategy first, notetaking is sometimes easier.)

The notes can now be sorted. I use scissors to cut the notes apart, making sure to leave meaningful phrases together. The students then manipulate the words and phrases from their notes into categories that make sense to them. As the categories evolve, students can place labels at the top of each category.

hairy bodies	hatch from eggs	some are poisonous
eight legs	eat insects	many varieties
spin webs	can bite people	
like moisture	many sizes	

To provide practice in inserting notes right into a category, I read some additional information to the students, ask them to take a note about it, and then ask them to decide immediately which category this new information belongs in.

Graphic organizer such as webs can also be helpful for this process. You could go through each note and ask the students to determine which part of the web the note is related to. Does it belong in foods, in habitat, in behaviors, or ?

This process of sorting helps students to realize that the purpose of notes is to gather like ideas together so that they can eventually write about what they have learned in an organized way.

Now if you move to cards or other notetaking ideas, the process and purpose are much clearer to the students.

Questioning as You Go

Reader _____ Text _____ Date _____

Good readers ask themselves questions while they read. They also ask questions of the text. While you read today, focus on your questions. Take time to wonder.

Before reading, I wonder about _____

_____

_____

_____

During reading, I wondered about:

_____

_____

In the text _____

_____

_____

The topic in general _____

_____

_____

After reading, I still wonder _____

_____

_____

_____

Summarizing

Good readers can summarize what they read in clear and concise terms. They can distill key ideas (Keene and Zimmerman 1996) and identify important details as well. When readers summarize, they need to reflect on the entire content and then find a way to restate the information without including too much detail.

I believe that children really benefit when I demonstrate summarizing for them. After read alouds, a content area exploration, or a shared text experience I often make statements such as: *If I were to summarize this, I need to think about:*

- keeping it brief
- hitting on the big, main ideas
- mentioning some supporting details
- sharing my personal perspectives. Did I make a connection? Was there a place in the text or a photograph that really caught my interest? Do I have questions about a statement or a desire to learn more about this topic?

After thinking aloud about the planning process, I would then do a retell and ask them to check me. Did I: Keep it brief, hit the big ideas, and so on?

Now when I ask students to summarize a passage, they have a frame. They see clearly the goal and are better able to generate meaningful summaries both orally and in writing.

Shandra Moss, a third-grade teacher from North Carolina, writes:

Read, Cover, Remember, Retell

Shandra Moss

My kids benefit from me modeling, but I realized that I was always doing all of the work. So . . . I tried *Read, Cover, Remember, Retell* (Hoyt 1999). That remember section caused a change. The students told me, "The remember part is the hardest, Mrs. Moss!" I encouraged them to keep trying because the "remember" part is also the most important. For the next several days, we worked on *Read, Cover, Remember, Retell*. They thought it was the best. They giggled and smiled the whole time. I think the giggles were the signs of "We got it!"

Barbara Milton, a reading specialist at May Whitney School in Lake Zurich, Illinois, writes:

Main Idea

Barbara Milton

Dear Linda,

To help students focus on ideas in a paragraph during guided reading, I begin by teaching *Read, Cover, Remember, and Retell.* They quickly learn to retell general content. At that point I begin to encourage them to tease out the main idea by having them flag it with a sticky note in the text. We then discuss the main idea and the details that support it.

With practice, my students have become more skilled at detecting the main idea and supportive details. The next step might involve using the flagged ideas to write a summary of what they have just read.

Sum It Up

Reader _____ Text _____ Date _____

Good readers take time to stop reading and think about what they have learned. As you read today, stop at the end of each page and think. What did I just learn? What is most important?

Page #_____   Sum It Up Notes

_____

_____

Page #_____   Sum It Up Notes

_____

_____

Page #_____   Sum It Up Notes

_____

_____

Page #_____   Sum It Up Notes

_____

_____

Page #_____   Sum It Up Notes

_____

_____

When you have finished reading, review your notes. If you were to tell someone what you learned, what would you say?

_____

_____

_____

Retelling

Preparing an Informational Retell

Version I

Reader _____ Title of Book _____ Topic _____

- Create an illustration that shows what you learned in this book. Create labels to show the important parts. You may want to add a caption too.

- Tell a partner about your illustration. Make sure your partner learns what you did. My partner's name is _____.

3. Write about your topic. Be sure to include the important ideas.

_____

_____

_____

_____

_____

Preparing an Informational Retell

Version II

Reader _____ Title of Book _____

Topic _____ Date _____

Prepare a retell of the important points in this book. Select several of the boxes below that will help you remember the key ideas. (You don't need to use all of the boxes.) In each of the boxes you select, you can choose to either draw a quick sketch or jot down your thinking. The goal is to use this sheet to help yourself prepare to retell the most important information from this reading.

Place a √ in the boxes you select.

❑ What was the main idea the author was trying to communicate?

❑ What else did you learn?

❑ If you were to write about this topic and tell just the most important parts, what would you include?

❑ What was the most interesting part of this book?

❑ If you were going to do further research on this topic, what would you want to learn?

❑ Did you think the author presented the information well? Why or why not?

Informational Retell

Reader _____ Book _____

Data Collected by: _____ Topic _____ Date _____

Unassisted Retell

Record in each box with tally marks or anecdotal notes.

   Please tell me about the book you just read. I will be listening for the main ideas as well as for interesting facts you include. I am also interested in what you thought about the book. Please feel free to point to the pictures and any parts of the text that will help you share your learning.

Main Ideas	Details	Use of Text Features

Questioning	Conclusions	Inferences

Connections	Mental Pictures

Assisted Retell

If the information provided above is sketchy, you may want to ask a few probing questions to elicit more from the reader. Try to keep your questions open-ended, such as: Can you tell more about how _____?
Were there any other points in the reading you found to be important? If you were going to tell your friend about this, is there anything else you would add? Were you able to make any connections while you were reading?

Retelling Rubric

Reader _____ Book _____

Topic _____ Date _____

6   The retell covered all main ideas and included an array of supporting details.

    The text was referenced in the retell. On page ___, it stated that ___.

    The text features were referenced, in the photo on page ___, it said ___.

    Beyond the text, extensions were offered that included logical conclusions, inferences, and ongoing questions on the topic.

4   The retell covered most main ideas and many supporting details.

    Either the text or text features were referenced, but not both.

    The retell had few extensions beyond the text such as logical conclusions, inferences, and ongoing questions.

2   The retell covered details but not main ideas.

    Facts were accurate.

    There was no reference to the text or text features.

    There were no text extensions.

1   The retell had inaccuracies. Information was minimal.

Rank-Ordering Information

While reading, have students list phrases that either describe the content they are reading or are phrases taken directly from the text. Make it clear that they want to select things they believe to be important to the topic.

After reading, cut the list apart into strips. Then begin evaluating and sorting strips into categories. They will find it easiest to pull out the most important and least important ideas first, leaving moderately important for last. Categories headings should read:

MOST IMPORTANT IDEAS	MODERATELY IMPORTANT IDEAS	LEAST IMPORTANT IDEAS

Then lead the class in a discussion. Some of the questions to consider: If we were to write a summary, which ideas are most helpful? Could we justify our opinions about "most important" ideas with something from the text? How does our ranking fit in with other readings we have done on this topic?

Michelle Khatewoda is a first-grade teacher in McMinnville, Oregon with the fire of a co-learner in her eyes. Michelle is one of those rare and precious teachers who is always thirsting for something new that will make a bigger difference faster for her students and is willing to go the extra mile (notice the hat in the picture) to ensure that her students are excited about learning.

A Guided Reading Lesson

Michelle Khatewoda

I introduced the nonfiction book *Ears* to a group of early readers. This particular group has difficulty attending to print. Although their errors are meaningful, they tend to make up the story based on the pictures and their memory of the book introduction. So I picked a fairly predictable and repetitive text so that we could focus on attending to the print. I chose to scale back my book introduction and not give very much support for the purpose of challenging this group to really focus on the print. As part of my brief introduction, we discussed the table of contents and the index. We talked about why nonfiction books have these resources and how we use them.

The boys struggled through the first read because they weren't looking at the text. They were still just making up text based on the pictures. After the first read, we regrouped and talked about why they had struggled so much. Each student told me the same thing: "I wasn't looking at the words." My first reaction (in my head) was

FIGURE 13.6 First-grade teacher Michelle Khatewoda engaging first graders with an informational text. Reading strategies are taught just as in a fiction guided reading experience.

"O.K. You can tell me what you should do. Why aren't you doing it???" I refrained from saying that thought out loud. Instead, I reminded them to use their fingers and to point to each word as they said it. If their finger wasn't pointing to a word, they couldn't say a word. We practiced that strategy on a couple pages. Then I had them continue on their own.

As I listened to them individually, I was pleased to see that they were using the one-to-one matching strategy and paying closer attention to the text. When they got stuck on a word, instead of making up something, they were getting their mouths ready to say the first sound. When they completed the second read, I could tell that they felt really pleased with themselves. We talked about what had made this read better than the first and how attending to the print helps us understand what we're reading so much more.

Most importantly, while they were busy learning about one-to-one correspondence, they learned a lot about the ears of various animals!

FIGURE 13.7 Christian is completely involved in the picture walk for the book *Ears*.

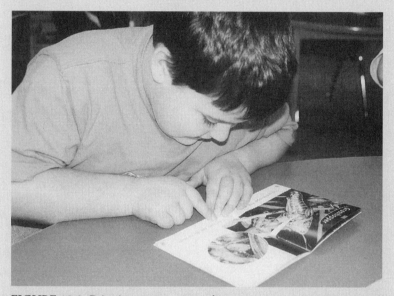

FIGURE 13.8 Brice is one-to-one matching.

FIGURE 13.9 Ms. K listening to Gaye's first read.

Wendy Autencio is an upper-grade teacher in McMinnville, Oregon. This upper-grade guided reading lesson shows the power of explicit teaching for students who have reached fluency. Guided reading brings fluent readers to higher levels of proficiency than they could attain on their own by demonstrating text features and scaffolding informational searching techniques.

Learning About Crocodiles, Learning About Text: Guided Reading with Upper Elementary-Age Students

Wendy Autencio

My five students gathered in a circle. They brought their own books to read for a five-minute warm-up.

I did book talks on several informational titles and then we voted on the one they would most like to read.

FIGURE 13.10 Book talks help students choose a book to read as their guided reading focus.

They chose a book on crocodiles so we made a chart listing the facts they already knew. This sparked a few discussions between the students. Some gathered their information from books that were previously read, while others talked about information gained from watching "The Crocodile Hunter" on television.

FIGURE 13.11 A chart of crocodile facts.

I thought we could go straight to the table of contents and select a section to read, but the students were so excited that they couldn't decide on a topic to read. So we proceeded to do a picture walk. This was amazing because they related the pictures to our chart of crocodile facts.

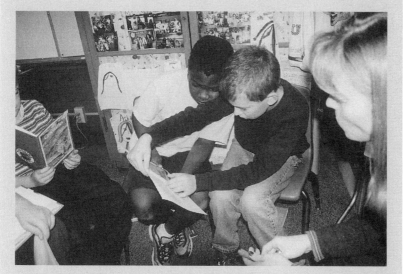

FIGURE 13.12 Locating the information using the table of contents.

FIGURE 13.13 Listing strategies and facts.

After looking at the pictures, we did a quick rundown on strategies for reading informational books and returned to the table of contents. We discussed that we could start on any chapter, and did not have to read the book in sequence since we were hunting for facts.

We looked at our chart, comparing it to the table of contents, then decided as a group to read a chapter on nesting since that is the one topic we gathered most information on when we were brainstorming at the beginning of the session.

We ended by preparing ourselves for the next day's lesson. We decided to do a reciprocal teaching lesson (see chapter on Reciprocal Teaching) as we continued to explore the book on crocodiles.

FIGURE 13.14 Reciprocal teaching in action. Photographs by Kathy Baird, Reading Recovery teacher–leader and staff developer in McMinnville, Oregon.

Shandra Moss, the third-grade teacher in North Carolina, shares her reflections on management strategies for guided reading from the view of a second-year teacher.

Building Interest in Informational Texts: Through the Eyes of a Second-Year Teacher

Shandra Moss

When children come in the morning, we have baskets of nonfiction texts, magazines, etc. available for independent reading and browsing. This gives them an extra fifteen to twenty minutes of reading each day and they really like it. I put out a baggy of bookmarks with comments like *Neat!*, *New Discovery!*, *I want to try this in my writing!*, and, of course, post-its for connections, etc. This time goes by really quickly as the students are so engaged.

FIGURE 13.15 Warming with informational selections.

My guided reading block runs 8:45–9:45 A.M. with three rotations of twenty minutes each. The students are divided into three groups so each child sees me for twenty minutes and has two literacy centers.

The literacy centers are organized to focus on reading, writing, and word work. Current centers include poetry, buddy reading, word work, and writing.

During guided reading one group read "Chew on This," a nonfiction article about gum all over the world (*National Geographic for Kids*). We read just about everything during guided reading!! They love nonfiction so much.

I am pleased that they have a tendency to find other materials on their own related to anything I teach that is nonfiction. Since they broaden their understanding of the topic through reading on their own, our discussions get better and better. The fact that they are empowered makes a difference in every minute of that time.

I modeled the *Two-Word Strategy* (see Hoyt, *Revisit, Reflect, Retell,* 1999) with these two groups. That is great for specific objectives and as a springboard for writing. I used it for Main Idea!!! Next week we are going to use the *Two-Word Strategy* for Author's Purpose and Author's Point of View with *Time for Kids*.

I am starting an integrated unit on Earth, Sun, and Moon Patterns. So, I will be tackling guided reading with the science text next.

The most important thing I am working on is time for sharing and reflection for the kids about how their reading is changing. It is hard to remember to do this. It feels like something that does not have immediate short-term results but will have big benefits over the long haul.

14

Multilevel Theme Sets
Support for Differentiating Instruction

As we face increasing levels of diversity in our classrooms, along with higher-stakes assessment, it is critical that we provide students with opportunities to read materials that are at their "just-right level" all day long.

It is time for textbooks to take their place as resources as we teach thematically focused units of study that integrate state standards in science, social studies, and health. When textbooks take the role of resources, instead of the central focus of curriculum, we can teach to the bigger more global understandings that are important to our lives as literate adults. We can follow student interests and create a tighter match to standards than any one textbook can provide. Most importantly, when we move beyond textbooks, we can teach students the content standards within materials that will also help them grow as readers. We can give them the opportunity to learn about the world while they develop skill as readers.

FIGURE 14.1 A multilevel theme set provides numerous reading choices at varying reading levels.

Multilevel theme kits are a support system to this kind of teaching. They provide a range of books on a focused topic, while providing a wide range of difficulty levels for reading. They also support cross-curricular connections as these kits make it easy to link guided reading instruction during language arts time to the units of study in science, social studies, and health. This is important as too many reading efforts switch from topic to topic, giving learners a light glossing of knowledge but no real depth in which concepts and language can develop. It is simply too hard for readers to keep all of the words in their heads when you switch from topic to topic.

When building a multilevel theme kit teachers ask themselves a range of questions:

1. What is this unit about? What are my goals?
2. Have I selected a unit that is broad enough that students with varying backgrounds will be able to connect and apply their prior knowledge? (Narrow units such as teddy bears rarely produce enough books to support all students in a classroom.)
3. Do these books match the state standard and the unit of study?
4. Have I collected books at a wide range of difficulty levels so all students can access the topic and still be reading at their just-right level?
5. Have I included some books on the topic in single copies for individual research and read alouds?
6. Have I included multiple copies of books at a range of levels so guided reading can be linked to our unit of study?
7. Have I included some books on tape and other supports that will enable students to experience books they are passionate about, even if those books are a bit above their reading level?
8. Is this multilevel theme set organized in such a way that other teachers can use it too?
9. Have there been any issues of our news magazine on this topic that could be added to the kit as additional resources?

It can be very helpful to use crates with hanging folders inside to organize your multilevel theme kits. The crate can be labeled with the topic and the folders filled with guided reading books, read aloud books, shared text ideas, and so on that support an integrated curriculum.

If you already have established a book room with a collection of resources for your school, you would simply need to survey your collection for books on thematic topics that match your standards and ensure that there is a wide range of difficulty levels represented in your collection along with enough breadth on the topic to really give the unit of study support. Once the kit is built, then the textbook can become a powerful resource. It is a place to look for additional information, a place to look for another perspective on the topic, and it will be easier to read because students already have some experience with the topic.

When students experience a unit of study that weaves a rich tapestry of whole class discussions, small group guided reading, and independent reading all focused around the same topic, they feel supported. They learn the content more effectively. They learn the language that surrounds and supports the unit of study.

Most importantly, after reading about a topic in resources that are at their own reading level, they have built prior knowledge and vocabulary. They will understand the content better and will have also improved their reading skills.

Jan McCall, Title I Literacy Facilitator, in Beaverton, Oregon has guided teams of teachers in constructing multilevel theme kits.

Multilevel Theme Kits in Action

Jan McCall

Many elementary students are confronted with science and social studies texts that are too complex for optimum learning (Allington 2001). One way to help students access content information at their reading level is to create kits containing sets of leveled books, usually nonfiction, that address a theme linked to science or social studies standards.

At McKinley Elementary in Beaverton, Oregon, a group of teachers organized a number of multilevel theme kits and created documents that listed connections to science standards as well as a focus on language arts standards for each set of books.

The kits represented a range of state and district standards and were built to be portable—easily carried to a classroom. With the kit are topic-related books in single copies for read alouds and multiple copies for guided reading.

Included with each book set is information on an index card that elaborates on the language arts standards with suggested teaching points, questioning strategies, and supports for English Language Learners. The cards are meant to be an ongoing record of the work done by all teachers using the kit. Teachers note teaching strategies, think aloud ideas, and follow-up activities so that others can benefit.

Teachers check the kits out from the school book room to support science lessons, as an alternative or supplement to using the science textbook, or for integrating language arts and science in a guided reading.

Multilevel Theme Set on Mammals

Level	Nonfiction/ Fiction	Title	Publisher	Science Content	Literature Focus
A	Nonfiction	*A Cat's Day*	Wright Group	Describe the relationship between the habitat and the animal	Literal comprehension
A	Nonfiction	*A Friend for Me*	Pacific	Compare and contrast difference between pets and wild animals	Inferential comprehension
B	Nonfiction	*My Horse*	Bebop	Compare and contrast difference between pets and wild animals	Literal comprehension
C	Nonfiction	*Baby Animal at Home*	Newbridge	Describe the relationship between the habitat and the animal	Literal comprehension
C	Nonfiction	*Everyone Eats*	Newbridge	Describe the relationship between the habitat and the animal	Literal comprehension
C	Nonfiction	*Koalas*	Rigby	Describe the relationship between the habitat and the animal	Inferential comprehension Literal comprehension
E	Nonfiction	*Polar Bears*	Wright Group	Describe how related animals have similar characteristics	Literary forms Literary comprehension
E	Fiction	*The Cat and the Mice*	Wright Group	Identify predator-prey relationships	Word meaning Literal comprehension
F	Nonfiction	*Cats*	Wright Group	Describe how related animals have similar characteristics	Evaluative comprehension Literal comprehension
G	Nonfiction	*Animals and Their Babies*	Newbridge	Distinguish between basic and nonessential needs of an organism	Locating information
G	Nonfiction	*Kittens*	Newbridge	Describe the life cycle of an animal	Locating information Literal comprehension

H	Nonfiction	*Big Bears*	Newbridge	Describe the relationship between the habitat and the animal	Locating information Inferential comprehension
H	Nonfiction	*Tails Can Tell*	Wright Group	Describe how related animals have similar characteristics	Evaluative comprehension Inferential comprehension
I	Nonfiction	*Gorilla*	Groset & Dunlap	Describe the relationship between the habitat and the animal	Evaluative comprehension Literal comprehension
J	Nonfiction	*Growl*	Scholastic	Describe the relationship between the habitat and the animal	Literal comprehension
K	Fiction	*Stellaluna*	Harcourt Brace	Compare and contrast bats to birds	Literary elements and devices Word meaning, evaluative comprehension
L	Nonfiction	*Hairy Little Critters*	Rigby	Identify how an animal's fur helps in adapting to environment	Locating information Word meaning
N	Nonfiction	*Call of the Wolves*	Ranger Rick	Describe how related animals have similar characteristics	Locating information Word meaning
N	Nonfiction	*How Do Animals Sleep?*	Ranger Rick	Distinguish between basic and nonessential needs of an organism	Locating information Word meaning
P	Nonfiction	*Winter Survival*	Rigby	Identify how an organism adapts to a specific environment	Locating information Evaluative comprehension
Q	Nonfiction	*Bats*	Ranger Rick	Distinguish between basic and nonessential needs of an organism	Word meaning Locating information

Multilevel Theme Set on Plants

Level	Title	Author	Publisher	Science Content	Reading Content	Nonfiction/Fiction
A	*The Smallest Tree*	P. Johnson	Rigby	Describe the life cycle of a tree. Compare and contrast an evergreen tree with a tree that does lose its leave such as an oak tree.	Literal comprehension Literary form	Nonfiction
B	*Growing*	M. Wyvill	Rigby	Understand the life cycle of a plant.	Locating information	Nonfiction
B	*A Little Seed*	J. Mellwain	Rigby	Describe basic needs of a plant. Understand the life cycle of a plant.	Literal comprehension Inferential comprehension	Fiction
C	*Leaves, Fruit, Seeds, and Roots*	J. Baxton	Learning Media	Describe characteristics that are similar and different between plants.	Literal comprehension	Fiction
D	*Dad's Garden*	H. Christie	Rigby	Explain and analyze the interdependence of organisms in their natural environment.	Inferential comprehension	Nonfiction
D	*In the Garden*	A. Smith	Rigby	Describe a habitat and the organisms that live there.	Inferential comprehension	Nonfiction
D	*In the Garden*	P. Cartwright	Rigby	Explain and analyze the interdependence of organisms in their natural environment.	Literal comprehension Inferential comprehension	Nonfiction
D	*Our Garden*	A. Statley	Rigby	Describe basic needs of a plant. Describe the effect humans have on plants.	Inferential comprehension Literary elements and devices	Fiction
D	*Pumpkin, Pumpkin*	J. Titherington	Scholastic	Describe the life cycle of plant.	Literal comprehension Inferential comprehension	Fiction
D	*Sally's Beans*	B. Randell	Rigby	Describe basic needs of a plant. Describe the life cycle of a plant.	Inferential comprehension	Fiction
D	*Food from the Plants*	C. Sinnatt	Rigby	Identify different parts of a plant and how humans use them.	Locating information—table of contents Literal comprehension	Nonfiction

Level	Title	Author	Publisher	Objective	Skill	Genre
E	Grow Seed Grow	L. Trumbauer	Newbridge	Describe the basic needs of a plant. Describe the life cycle of a plant.	Literal comprehension—sequence	Nonfiction
E	How to Grow a Sunflower	S. Karavis	Rigby	Describe basic needs of a seed. Describe the relationship between a plant and a human.	Locating information—table of contents and index, captions	Nonfiction
E	Max and the Little Plant	A. Smith	Rigby	Describe basic needs of a plant.	Inferential comprehension	Fiction
E	My Plant	P. Barrios	Rigby	Describe basic needs of a plant. Describe characteristics and structures of a plant.	Literal comprehension / Inferential comprehension / Evaluative	Nonfiction
E	What's Alive?	L. Trumbauer	Newbridge	Explain why a tree is alive—describe basic needs.	Inferential comprehension—compare and contrast what's alive and what's not	Nonfiction
F	In the Park	G. Meadows	Rigby	Describe a habitat (plant) and the organisms (animals) that live there.	Literal comprehension	Nonfiction
F	Jamall's City Garden	L. Washington	Rigby	Describe basic needs of a plant.	Locating information / Literal comprehension / Evaluative comprehension	Nonfiction
F	Sarah's Seed	M. Watts	Rigby	Recognize that organisms are produced by living organisms of similar kind.	Inferential comprehension	Fiction
G	The Amazing Popple Seed	J. Cowley	Rigby	Compare and contrast a real tree to the pretend trees in the story.	Literal comprehension—sequencing	Fiction
G	Growing a Plant	R. Jenkins	Rigby	Describe life cycle of a plant.	Locating information / Literal comprehension	Nonfiction
G	How New Plants Grow	C. Walker	Modern Curriculum	Describe basic plant structures and their functions. Compare and contrast how different plants reproduce. Describe the life cycle.	Literal comprehension / Locating information	Nonfiction

(continues)

Multilevel Theme Set on Plants (*continued*)

Level	Title	Author	Publisher	Science Content	Reading Content	Nonfiction/ Fiction
G	*Jessie's Flower*	R. Bacon	Rigby	Explain and analyze the interdependence of plants in their natural environment.	Literal comprehension—sequencing Inferential comprehension	Fiction
G	*Look in the Garden*	J. Giles	Rigby	Classify plant—fruit, vegetable, etc.	Literal comprehension—sequencing	Fiction
G	*T.J.'s Tree*	M. Vaughan	Rigby	Describe basic needs of a tree. Infer the life cycle of a tree.	Literal comprehension—sequence Inferential comprehension	Fiction
G	*Terrific Trees*	M. Manhart	Rigby	Describe and analyze the effect humans have on trees—ecosystem, recycling. Describe the relationship between plants and humans.	Locating information Literal comprehension Word meaning	Nonfiction
H	*Sally's Surprise Garden*	M. Gibson	Rigby	Describe the basic needs of a living plant.	Inferential comprehension	Fiction
H	*The Wheelbarrow Garden*	A. Smith	Rigby	Describe basic needs of a plant.	Inferential comprehension	Fiction
J	*Diary of a Sunflower*	C. Evans	Rigby	Describe basic plant structures and their functions. Describe the basic needs of a living plant. Describe the life cycle.	Locating information—graphs and captions Literary form	Nonfiction
J	*Trees*	R. Vaughan	Rigby	Describe the life cycle. Describe characteristics that are similar and different between various trees. Describe the relationship between trees and humans—why trees are important to humans.	Literal comprehension Inferential comprehension Evaluative comprehension—author's purpose	Nonfiction

Level	Title	Author	Publisher	Description	Skills	Genre
L	Trees Belong to Everyone	D. Noonan	Rigby	Describe and analyze the effect of species including humans on an ecosystem.	Evaluative comprehension Inferential comprehension	Fiction
M	Dear Diary	J. Press	Rigby	Describe the basic needs of a living plant. Describe the life cycle of a plant.	Literal comprehension Word meaning	Nonfiction
M	Nature's Celebration	P. Garland	Rigby	Describe a habitat (plant) and the organisms (animals) that live there.	Word meaning Inferential comprehension	Nonfiction
N	Animal, Plant or Mineral?	D. Drew	Rigby	Categorize and sort various organisms according to their structures.	Inferential comprehension	Nonfiction
N	Green Thumb	C. Hosking	Rigby	Describe the basic needs of a living plant. Describe basic plant structures and their functions. Describe the process of photosynthesis.	Locating information Literal comprehension Word meaning	Nonfiction

Multilevel Theme Set on Growing and Changing

Subtheme	Titles	A–C	D–G	H–K	L–S	Series	Publisher
Plants Grow and Change	Making a Garden	X				Foundations	Wright Group
	Making Raisins	X				Windows on Literacy	National Geographic
	Flowers	X				Karen Hoenecke	Kaeden Books
	Gardens Are Great		X			Safari Magazine	Mondo
	How to Grow a Plant		X			Visions	Wright Group
	The Popcorn Book			X		Reading Unlimited	Celebration Press
	Growing Radishes and Carrots			X		BookShop	Mondo
	The Magic School Bus Plants Seeds				X	Joanna Cole and Bruce Degen	Scholastic
Animals Grow and Change	Baby Animals	X				Reading Corner Series	Dominie
	Frogs	X				Twig Series	Wright Group
Communities Grow and Change	Making a Road	X					Sundance
People Grow and Change	Before I Go To School	X				Storyteller	Shortland
	The Art Lesson				X	Tomie DePaola	Putnam
Creating Change	Making Raisins	X				Windows on Literacy	National Geographic
	Baking a Cake		X				Sundance
	Experiments with Water				X	Bryan Murphy	Scholastic

Title		Series	Publisher
Let's Make Something New	X	Discovery Links	Newbridge
Making Pancakes	X	Carousel Readers	Dominie
Making Paper	X	Little Green Reader Series	Sundance
How to Cook Scones	X	Bookshelf	Scholastic
How to Make a Mud Pie	X	Little Readers	Houghton Mifflin
How to Make Salsa	X	BookShop	Mondo
Let's Bake	X	Discovery Links	Newbridge
Making Lemonade	X		Sundance
Making Electricity	X		Sundance
How Is a Crayon Made?	X	Charles Oz	Scholastic
How to Grow Crystals	X	Bookshop Series	Mondo
How to Make a Cake	X	Foundations	Wright Group
Science—Just Add Salt	X	Sandra Markle	Scholastic

Weather Changes

Title		Series	Publisher
Today's Weather Is . . .		BookShop	Mondo
Fall	X	Discovery Links	Newbridge
Rain	X	Reading Corners Series	Dominie
Seasons	X	Discovery World	Rigby
Make a Cloud, Measure the Wind		Foundations	Wright Group

15

Literature Circles
with Informational Texts

Literature circles are a much loved component of literacy learning for many students. The opportunity to explore text in the company of good friends is a highly satisfying experience that many adults also enjoy in the format of adult book clubs.

When literature circle structures are connected to informational texts, students have the benefit of a social structure they love, the shared thinking of their peers, and deepened content knowledge.

Key Understandings About Informational Literature Circles

Be clear about your purpose for conducting literature circles. Circles enhance and deepen understanding, build motivation for reading, and expand oral language development. It is critical to plan for additional instructional in strategic reading behaviors. A circle can deepen comprehension but it does not teach reading strategies.

There is no one "right" way to engage in literature circles. The structure needs to evolve in response to your students and your personal teaching style. If you choose to use roles, remember that the roles are just a scaffold for the discussion and not the long-term goal. In many cases, roles can be dropped as groups gain proficiency.

Demonstrations are the key to success.

- Spend a lot of time "thinking aloud" about texts to show your students how you look more deeply into a text.
- Guide your class through in-depth discussions.
- Try a fishbowl where a small group engages in a discussion with you while the others observe.

- Invite students to help make lists of terrific informational text questions.
- Your read aloud times and the minilessons you conduct at the opening of each circle are critical to improving the quality of discussions and to your students' growth as readers.

Move slowly toward independence.

- Consider a two-step approach in which all members of a circle share the same role or have the same task, such as marking VIP (Very Important Points) with sticky notes before moving to individual responsibilities.
- Use small tape recorders to record discussions so that you can listen to them later. Barry Hoonan, educator from Bainbridge Island, Washington suggests that the tape recorders improve participation and raise levels of responsibility. Even if you only listen to bits and pieces of conversations while driving in your car, the students really notice when you make comments like: "While listening to the tape from yesterday's discussion, I noticed that Erin. . . ."

Utilize a wide variety of informational texts (newspapers, magazines, informational poems, textbooks, picture books, resource books, and so on).

- Build structures that ensure students come to the circle *prepared* to discuss. Post clear expectations for preparing. Give them a task to complete before the circle that may include reading, writing, marking key points, or summarizing.
- Make adjustments for struggling readers (finding materials at their just-right level on the same topic, paired reading, listening to the story before reading independently, having help preparing for the conversation, and so on).

The Teacher's Role
"To quietly guarantee the success of the discussion."

Key Points for Success

GUIDE STUDENTS TO ELABORATE AND EXTEND THEIR THINKING

"Can you tell us a little more?"

"Can you think of a reason that might have happened?"

"What an interesting thought. Can anyone else link up to that?"

"Soliz, do you have anything to add to that?"

"Making connections is so important. Can anyone else think of a connection to the story?"

"What can you find in the text that supports Caitlyn's idea?"

VALIDATE AND AFFIRM PROCEDURES

"Nice link up to Miguel's comments."

"Thank you for being patient, Alvarito. Allan has noticed your signal that you want to respond. I will help him to remember to give you a turn as soon as he is finished sharing his idea."

"Your comments show that you have really thought about this . . ."

"I have noticed that you are waiting until a topic is completely finished before moving on to another idea."

"We have five minutes left. What other thoughts do you have about this topic?"

ENCOURAGE USE OF EVIDENCE

"Can we find something in the story to support that idea?"

"How lucky for you that you had a personal experience to help you understand the story."

"Is there evidence for that anywhere?"

"I wonder if someone can find something in the text to help us? When you find it, let's all read it together."

ASSIST IN CLARIFYING IDEAS

"I think I heard you say _____. Did I summarize that well?"

"I am not sure I understand. Can you say that in another way or tell us a bit more?"

"Sometimes it is a bit hard to hear. Could you repeat that thought?"

"Oh, so you are saying that _____. What do the rest of you think?"

SUPPORT PARTICIPATION FROM ALL STUDENTS

"Is there anyone else who has a thought about this?"

"Is there anyone else who would like to respond to James' question?"

"Majon, your ideas are important to us. Please let us know when you are ready to share your thoughts."

"How are we doing today at giving everyone a turn to talk?"

Stimulating Discussion

Partner #1 _____ Partner #2 _____ Date _____

With a partner, read the passage assigned by your teacher or selected by you to match the unit of study. Think of two questions about the text that would *stimulate* conversation.

#1 _____

_____

_____

_____

#2 _____

_____

_____

_____

Meet with another partner pair. Share your questions with each other.

Which questions would you agree are most likely to stimulate deep conversations on this topic?

_____

_____

Bring your questions to the whole group and be ready to discuss your reading.

Literature Circle Scoring Guide

This scoring guide is meant to stimulate an oral interaction that asks group members to consider these questions and respond to each about how their group functioned. The goal is to use this reflection as a lead-in to goal setting as groups strive to improve the quality of their teamwork and conversations.

Today in our group . . .

	(5) Everyone was awesome					(0) It was a hard day
Everyone contributed	5	4	3	2	1	0
We stayed on task	5	4	3	2	1	0
We worked as a team	5	4	3	2	1	0
We kept eye contact	5	4	3	2	1	0
We were active listeners	5	4	3	2	1	0
There was a lot of piggybacking in our conversation	5	4	3	2	1	0
We justified our opinions with examples from the book	5	4	3	2	1	0

Our goal for next time is to improve _____

_____

_____

_____

Amy Anderson, a fifth-grade teacher from McMinnville, Oregon writes about her work with informational literature circles.

Informational Literature Circles

Amy Anderson

As a first-year teacher, I was a little unsure how to facilitate a nonfiction literature unit. Since the students did not seem eager to read nonfiction books on their own, I first tried to expose them to the topics that I had chosen for them to read.

For one group, I introduced a realistic fiction novel to get them hooked on the topic. I chose *Number the Stars* by Lois Lowry to precede an information book on World War II.

For another group, I chose a nonfiction book based on their passion for Early Civilizations during an earlier social studies unit. They had enjoyed the unit a great deal and had learned a lot, so I selected *Mummies, Bones and Body Parts* for their literature circle.

The last book I chose for my nonfiction unit was *The Great Fire*. I selected this because it was a Newberry Award Winner and the students in this group were a good match for the language complexities of this book.

To begin the unit, we talked as small groups about our prior knowledge on topics related to our books. We looked through the pictures to make predictions about new information that might be included and to list challenges we thought we might be prepared to face in each text.

I chose to have them do very little written response to keep them focused on reading and discussion of their topics.

As in fiction literature circles, the students met in their groups and decided on the number of pages they would read each day. They took complete ownership of what and how they would read each section of the text. Their enthusiasm was contagious. Their hesitation about informational books dissolved and they were begging me for more time at the end of each session.

After many student-led discussions, I could tell that my students had gained an appreciation for nonfiction. Our informational literature circles were a hit.

FIGURE 15.1

FIGURE 15.2

Amy guides a prereading discussion to activate and build prior knowledge for each book and then participates as students scan the text for quotes to back up their opinions.

FIGURE 15.3 While students read silently preparing for their informational literature circles, Amy conferences with a student to monitor use of meaning-seeking strategies.

FIGURE 15.4 Discussions were punctuated with skimming and scanning as students searched for specific points to use in justifying their thinking. The discussions were amazing.

Photographs by Kathy Baird, Staff Developer, McMinnville, Oregon.

16

Move Over Guided Reading
Reciprocal Teaching Comes Back

Reciprocal teaching, originally developed by Annmarie Palincsar and Ann Brown, is a powerful support system for building and enhancing comprehension. I have found it to be highly successful with students in all grades and especially appreciate reciprocal teaching's ability to facilitate both language use and content area understanding.

Reciprocal teaching was developed to engage small groups of readers in four essential reading processes: predicting, clarifying, questioning, and summarizing. The goal is to teach readers how to read reflectively, challenge themselves to think more deeply, and to use group interaction to enhance everyone's learning.

RECIPROCAL TEACHING STEPS

Predict

Clarify

Question

Summarize

Different from guided reading in which the teacher is always present in the group, reciprocal teaching is a model that can include the teacher as a group member but can also be a time when students support each other without the intervention of the teacher.

Model Reciprocal Processes During Read Alouds

During read alouds I stop often to refer to a poster of the four processes (as above) and use thinking aloud to model how I predict, clarify confusing ideas, and ask personal questions. I try to make my thinking as transparent as possible so the students can better understand my conscious effort to use the strategies as tools in helping myself understand the content I am reading. As I think aloud, I also make it clear to the students which of the strategies I am applying.

While reading from a passage on Sharks, I might stop reading, point to the boldface type and say: "I can *predict* that this section is on the eating habits of the shark because this boldface heading says: Dinner for the Shark."

SAMPLE QUESTIONS/STEMS

"What do you think the next part will be about?"

"What clues is the author giving us about the next section?"

"Based on _____ (a clue), I predict that . . ."

"The title/heading makes me think this will be about _____."

"The picture suggests that this page may include information on _____."

A little later in the reading, I might stop reading, point to the word *question* on the chart and wonder: "I have a *question* here. I am puzzled by the fact that the shark has to turn up its nose to expose its rows of teeth. I want to know how it moves that long nose up and pulls the mouth forward. I could even make my question sound like a question on a test."

Why does the shark turn up its nose?

SAMPLE QUESTIONS/STEMS

"Who is _____?"

"Why is _____ important?"

"How is _____ an example of _____?"

"What is most important about _____?"

"What is your opinion of _____?"

"I wonder _____ . . ."

"I'd like to know more about _____."

To demonstrate clarifying, I might stop reading and say: "I need to stop for a minute to *clarify* my thinking about this. I think the author means that the shark pushes its mouth forward so the mouth is at the front of the body instead of underneath so it is easier to catch its prey. I am going to re-read to clarify my thinking and try to understand if that is what the author means." "I need to clarify the meaning of the word *thrust*. I am going to re-read this sentence to see if the context will help and I am going to look again at the picture."

SAMPLE QUESTIONS/STEMS

"I don't understand the part about _____."

"A word or phrase I don't understand is _____."

"I am not sure the author was clear about _____."

"If I could ask the author about this, I would want clarification of _____."

"What is a _____?"

"What does _____ mean?"

To model summarizing, I might say: "I am going to stop for a moment and *summarize* what I know so far. I have learned that . . ."

SAMPLE QUESTIONS/STEMS

"The main idea of this section is _____."

"This section is mostly about _____."

"I learned that _____."

"The topic sentence suggests that _____."

"The author's message is focused on _____."

For each step of the process, I would point to the chart and be certain the students knew which of the four steps I was modeling.

This explicit modeling of the processes and continual referencing of the chart gives students the language to describe the strategies they are applying as thinkers and as readers. They can see during the modeling that these are steps that assist even an adult reader in elevating levels of understanding during reading, and they are able to observe the cyclical nature of the steps. With each new section of text, I repeat the steps of predicting, clarifying, questioning, and summarizing to ensure that students know how readers use these steps over and over again while reading a single passage.

Interactive Read Alouds

As students demonstrate that they understand the steps, I start engaging them in an interactive read aloud format where they can become more involved in applying the strategies but leave the responsibility for the reading to me. The goal is to engage students in actively using predicting, questioning, clarifying, and summarizing while I am there to guide and coach their efforts. This works well when I read an informational text aloud but I find more energy is created in the group if I place the text on the overhead or use a Big Book so the students can see the visual supports on the page.

Predicting in an Interactive Read Aloud

To begin, I ask for volunteers to *predict* ideas that they think will be covered on this page. Students get very used to making predictions in fiction but often forget to utilize that powerful strategy when reading informational text. Volunteers might say something like: "I predict from the pictures that this section is about the inside workings of a volcano." Or, "I can predict that this section is identifying a cause for the Civil War." Or, "I predict from the boldface headings that this entire page is going to focus on ways to protect the earth." Or, "I predict that there is going to be a comparison coming because the author starts the next sentence with: " 'The difference between . . .' " I encourage students to use picture clues, the title, boldface headings, and signal words (which give clues to the author's intent) as they make their predictions.

Clarifying Words and Ideas in an Interactive Read Aloud

Clarifying could be emphasized in an interactive read aloud by reminding the students that to *clarify* is to make something more clear, more understandable. Clarification might be about an idea or even a word that is confusing or unknown.

I find that for some students visualization can support clarification. They might close their eyes, listen closely to the passage as it is read, and then share their visualization with a partner. As students communicate about their visualizations, points of confusion and differing understandings are often shared, providing an authentic reason to return to the text to re-read and clarify. As the visualizations are shared, I often ask them to reflect on a specific word from the passage. "As you were visualizing, how did you see the action of *thrusting* in your mind's eye? I am going to read it again. Please think closely about that word and what it means in this paragraph. How might we work together to clarify the meaning of that word? Are there any other words we could use instead of thrusting?"

Supporting Questions During an Interactive Read Aloud

The interactive read aloud offers a powerful time to gather the questions the students generate. It is essential that students clearly understand that *questioning* is a hallmark of good readers. This is not a sign of incompetent confusion, but rather a sign that a reader is actively thinking while reading. As shown above, I might stop my read aloud midstream, point to the word *question* on the chart . . . and say, "Please turn to your partner and share an 'I Wonder' question about the topic we are reading." Or "Please take a moment to think of a question we might encounter if there were to be a test on this section of the reading."

I often use a T-chart to collect their questions. On one side I write I Wonder questions they generate. These are usually questions students

I Wonder Questions	Questions That Could Appear on a Test About This Passage
I wonder if the shark was much different in prehistoric times?	Name three key parts of the shark's respiratory system. Why does the shark need to move its nose to eat?

feel aren't answered by the text. On the other side of the chart, I have the students create "test"-style or "teacher"-style questions about the section we just read.

Practice *Summarizing* During Interactive Read Alouds

As in the other steps, the interactive read aloud can provide practice in learning to stop and summarize after each section of information. Traditional summaries are conducted at the completion of reading. In reciprocal teaching, students summarize frequently during the reading of a passage. "What are the most important ideas in this section? What do you think the author would most want us to remember?" are reflections that occur at the end of each section.

Solidifying Understanding

Through interactive read alouds, I can solidify understandings, reteach as necessary, and encourage students of all achievement levels to gain confidence with the process. Throughout the modeling stage, I am careful to identify the strategy being used by referring to the chart and by using descriptors for my behavior. "I am going to stop reading now and *summarize*." I want to be very sure that they have language to label the process so they can discuss the strategies as well as the content and are able to separate the processes in their heads. It is essential that students are clear about the differences between predicting, clarifying, questioning, and summarizing.

Shifting Responsibility

One of the hallmarks of reciprocal teaching is the shifting of responsibility from the teacher to group members. In full implementation, small reciprocal groups meet independently with group members taking turns with the role of Discussion Leader.

To prepare students for independence with their groups, I begin asking students to lead the interactive read alouds. In a kindergarten or first-grade classroom, I would make a sign that says Discussion Leader and invite a student to stand next to me as I read from a Big Book. My support to that student might include prompts such as: "Mr. Discussion

Leader, what does the chart tell us to do first? Predict? Please call on someone to make a prediction about this section. Mr. Discussion Leader, what should we do next?"

As I shift responsibility for following the steps to the students, I coach and encourage but consciously try to step back. My goal at this stage is to read to them, observe their proficiency in using the strategies, and try to intervene as little as possible as Discussion Leaders take turns guiding us through short passages. I may need to slip back into some modeling and more explicit coaching, but I then try to quickly return responsibility to the students, and return to my role of observer.

All of this modeling and guided practice takes time, but it is so worthwhile. With adequate amounts of modeling the students truly begin to internalize the strategies and to see how the strategies improve understanding.

Shifting to Small Groups

Once the students understand the strategies, and the way a Discussion Leader guides them through the four steps with a short portion of text before inviting the next Discussion Leader to continue, I model a small group interaction. I often use a fishbowl format and have one small group meet with me while the other students circle around to watch and listen. Then, I can engage the whole class in a discussion of what they observed, what went well, and what a group might do to ensure success while working without the presence of the teacher. During this time I again reinforce the understanding that the four steps are repeated over and over again with each small section of print. I want the readers to be very clear that good readers don't just ask questions and summarize at the end of their reading, they do it over and over again throughout the text.

A second step might be to have a group meet in the fishbowl without me. I then become a member of the audience. The ultimate goal is to have students meeting in small groups, working their way through passages, and supporting one another in reaching new heights in understanding while I, the teacher, circulate and support as needed. To facilitate independence I provide each group with a poster listing the four steps in the process and remind the groups that the leader carries responsibility to ensure each speaker identifies the part of the process being utilized. Because of the extensive modeling done during read alouds, students understand that they will take turns being Discussion Leader with each person guiding the group through a short passage. They also understand that their goal is to work as a team to problem solve and get as much meaning as they can from the passage.

THE DISCUSSION LEADER

- Keeps the conversation moving
- Reminds group members to identify the part of the process they are using
- Encourages everyone to contribute
- Selects the stopping point (for emergent readers this may be a two-page layout, for more mature readers, this may be a boldface heading or some other natural break)
- Selects a recorder to collect important ideas and challenges

As a safety net, I provide a brightly colored card to each group. When there is a word that no member of the group can decipher, or a point of confusion in the text that the group cannot unravel, they record the page number and the problem on the card. As I circulate, I try to notice activity on a card, but I also try not to rescue them too quickly. I have learned that, given time to read on past a challenging point, students often glean enough information that they can resolve the problem themselves. So, I watch and observe that group closely. If they resolve their challenge, they cross the item off on the card. If the item is not crossed off within a few minutes, I join the group and provide assistance.

At the end of each reciprocal teaching session, I always spend a bit of time debriefing on two levels. (1) What did we learn today about the content? (2) How well did our process work today? What did we do well? What improvements might we make next time?

Reflections

- The role of prior knowledge is critical in any interaction with print. To ensure success with reciprocal teaching as in any other reading interaction, I take time before reading to activate prior knowledge and ensure that the students have a strong foundation in the concepts that will be addressed. If the students were to read a passage on bees, I might start by asking what they know about bees, about experiences with bees, and perhaps even bring in some honey for the group to taste. This concept of frontloading concepts, vocabulary, and content before reading is addressed in an earlier portion of this book but must be remembered for all interactions with informational text.

- Primary students benefit from reciprocal teaching as much as their more proficient elders! With the most emergent learners, we use Big Books and take turns being Discussion Leader as in the interactive read aloud. I serve as their secretary to record key points and questions. As soon as they demonstrate an understanding of the process, I shift reciprocal teaching into guided reading. Now, in a small group format, I can support individuals or reteach steps in the process while we are practicing book handling skills and concepts of print. With the most emergent students, I find that they can follow the reciprocal steps very naturally even if they just work with the pictures to predict, question, clarify, and summarize.

• Reciprocal teaching strategies work well in fiction! Try it with a picture book or a novel for variety.

• Many teachers find that inserting reciprocal teaching sequences into the time normally set aside for guided reading adds interest and a break from usual routines. Other teachers find that using guided reading during language arts time and reciprocal teaching during content area time brings another small group interaction into the day, increasing student responsibility, engagement, and learning!

• Try Literacy Frames to get a bit more muscle from the point where students clarify words. I ask each student to point out an interesting word and guide their group in framing it with a Literacy Frame. This brings everyone's visual attention to the word and increases the likelihood that the word will be remembered. Literacy Frames are very supportive of students who are challenged by attention as it brings their visual attention directly to the point of discussion.

• I find that many students benefit from having the steps of reciprocal teaching typed onto cards that they can flip as they move through the steps of reciprocal teaching. These cards increase engagement as every student can easily follow the process and I find that struggling students participate more fully when they have the cards to support their thinking.

Reciprocal Cards Version I:
Focus on the Process

Card 1

Prediction. Please get ready to read to _____. (Name a stopping point.) Please remember to use the pictures, bold-face type, and your prior knowledge.

Card 2

Who would like to share the first prediction?

Card 3

Would you like to read silently or in unison for this passage?

(Not round robin!)

Reciprocal Cards Version I:
Focus on the Process (*continued*)

Card 4

Clarifying Words. Were there any words you thought were interesting or had questions about?

Card 5

Clarifying Ideas. Were there any ideas you thought were interesting or that you found confusing?

Card 6

Questioning: Did you have any "I Wonder. . . ?" questions in this passage? What are some questions we might find on a test about this passage?

continues

Reciprocal Cards Version I:
Focus on the Process (*continued*)

Card 7

Summarizing: Please think about the passage for a moment and prepare to share what you learned.
(Wait . . .) Who would like to start?

Card 8

The next Discussion Leader will be _____.

(The leader names a natural stopping point in the text. For emergent readers this may be a two-page layout. For more mature readers, this may be a boldface heading or some other natural break.)

As students gain proficiency with the process I begin to have higher expectations of their communication about the text. The following set of cards is designed to scaffold communication and support full participation from all students.

Reciprocal Cards Version II: Focus on Conversations

Card 1

Predicting

I predict _____

The picture suggests that _____

I think the next section will be about _____

Based on (a clue in the text), I predict that _____

The heading for this section makes me think that _____

_____

I am making a connection that makes me think that _____

_____

continues

Reciprocal Cards Version II:
Focus on Conversations (*continued*)

Card 2

Clarifying

I wonder what the author meant when he said _____

_____

As I try to visualize this, I realize I am confused about

_____

I wish the author could tell us why _____

_____

One word/phrase I do not understand is _____

_____

I'd like to insert the word _____ to make this clearer.

This part was confusing. I looked at the picture, re-read, and _____ to clarify.

Reciprocal Cards Version II:
Focus on Conversations (*continued*)

Card 3

Questioning

I wonder _____

I'd like to know more about _____

Why is _____ important?

What is your opinion of _____?

How does this compare to _____?

What is the most important information in this section?

_____

continues

Reciprocal Cards Version II:
Focus on Conversations (*continued*)

Card 4

Summarizing

The key information in this section is _____

This section was mostly about _____

The main point was _____

The author's message was _____

The topic sentence mentioned _____

I think our summary should include _____

Part Four
Write All About It

The best nonfiction writing—and research—begins with a writer's passionate curiosity about a subject.

Joanne Portalupi

17

Modeled, Shared, and Interactive Writing of Informational Texts

During modeled writing, as during read aloud time, the teacher writes while the class watches. This writing may be done on a chart, on the overhead, or anywhere clearly visible to the students. The goal is to demonstrate fluent, factual writing while thinking aloud about how the text is being constructed. When modeled writing is based on communicating information, it is a perfect time to show students how to organize information, how to label drawings, make a key point, or show how to create headings that support the reader in getting the main idea of the passage.

Regie Routman (in *Conversations*, 2000) describes modeled writing as writing out loud. This is a wonderful reminder that it is not a silent effort but rather one in which the teacher is trying to make the processes of choosing a form, selecting ideas, generating illustrations and sentences, as transparent as possible to the students.

The products of modeled writing can provide outstanding samples for a wide range of text forms that can be saved over time. I like to keep my modeled writing selections as a long-term resource to students. If I am writing at the overhead, I simply make a photocopy and place it into a three-ring binder. If I am writing on chart paper with primary students, then I would collect various modeled writing samples and create a Big Book. The goal is to have a ready resource of models a student can turn to for reminders about various informational text forms. To make this resource as useful as possible, I keep a list of the forms that I model to assist my long-term planning. I also make a conscious effort to remind students to use the resource. When a student decides to write a persuasive letter, for example, I easily refer that student to the modeled persuasive letter in the notebook as a model to use in planning the piece.

Some of the writing processes I model follow.

PROCESSES TO MODEL

Think aloud about what you already know on the topic

Locating information; using resource books to gather ideas

Selecting key points to include

Using an illustration to collect data

Using a graphic organizer to collect data

Turning your data into interesting, inviting writing

Re-reading to ensure you are making sense

Checking to see if there is enough detail to keep the reader interested

How to get started writing

FORMS FOR MODELED WRITING

Personal letters (perhaps to share what you learned on an information topic)

Letters to the editor

Letters to a public official with the purpose of persuading

Directions for assembling something

Recipes

A manual for operating something

Informational descriptions

Informational narratives (turn the life cycle of a frog into a first-person narrative)

TEXT FEATURES TO INCLUDE IN MODELED WRITING

Labels on pictures

Titles

Captions

Headings

Boldface or italicized words

References

Table of contents

Index

Glossary

Picture glossary

Cross-section drawing

Comparison drawing

Shared Writing

With shared writing, there is a combination of teacher modeling and student input. The purposes can be to provide models for writing as in modeled writing, but students become *active* participants. Shared writing provides an opportunity to:

- Demonstrate a variety of forms for writing informational text
- Provide guided practice for all phases of the writing process
- Support engagement with a variety of informational text forms
- Build enthusiasm through shared participation in the crafting of a text

A shared writing looks much like language experience. Students generate ideas about the topic, wording, which text features to include, and so on. Even though you are doing all of the writing, students provide input about the content of each sentence such as where visuals such as diagrams or charts would enhance the meaning of a text. While you guide their thinking, you could also stretch them by suggesting a glossary entry to support their work or ask them to try for stronger verbs and adjectives.

Wall stories and innovations on text are often generated through shared writing experiences. (See Chapter 5 on emergent readers for more information.)

SHARED WRITING OFFERS INVITATIONS TO:

Build enthusiasm for writing

Demonstrate text forms

Teach skills in context

Teach reading/writing strategies

Think aloud about topic, word choice

Show how to stretch and hear the sounds in words

Demonstrate revision

Demonstrate editing

Engage in self-questioning during writing

Create a list of informational text features to place in a writing center (table of contents, glossary)

Connect to science, social studies, and math concepts

Teach minilessons based on observations of student writing

Interactive Writing

In interactive writing students "share the pen" with teacher guidance. Interactive writing on informational topics gives teachers and children opportunities to share responsibility for developing informational text forms and to reflect on content knowledge. In *Interactive Writing and Interactive Editing* (2001) by Schwartz, Klein and Shook, interactive writing is defined as "A teaching method in which children and teacher negotiate what they are going to write and then share the pen to construct a message." The students negotiate and come to agreement on wording of the text and title. The teacher writes down their ideas so their words are precisely maintained, then learners begin the process of sharing the pen to craft the text. With teacher guidance, one student may write a letter or a phoneme in a word while another may be asked to write an entire word. The process can be completed with a whole class or in a small group setting.

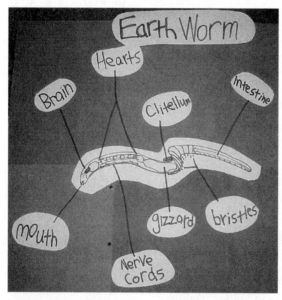

FIGURE 17.1 This cross-section diagram of the internal organs of an earthworm was constructed through interactive writing as part of a study on Life in Our Backyard.

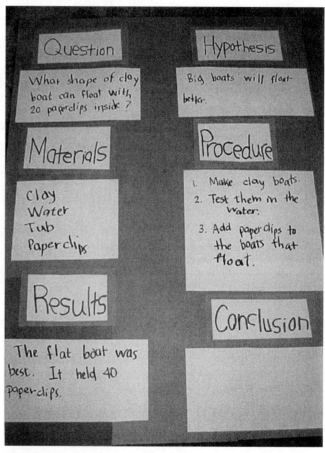

FIGURE 17.2 Interactive writing caught the essence of a scientific experiment showing steps from developing the question through hypothesis and procedure.

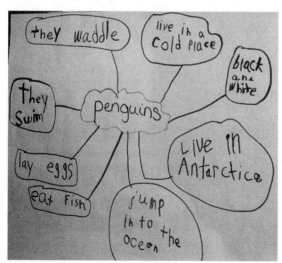

FIGURE 17.3 First graders used interactive writing to develop a web reflecting their study of penguins. Photo by Kathy Baird, Michelle Khatewoda's classroom, McMinnville, Oregon.

Interactive writing, like modeled and shared writing, is a powerful opportunity to heighten learner knowledge of content and forms for informational writing (McCarrier, Pinnell, and Fountas 2000).

Interactive Writing for Fluent Readers and Writers

Interactive writing offers strong support systems for upper elementary students too. Their interactive explorations of informational text could include descriptive writing, directions, persuasive pieces, story problems, collaboratively built travel brochures, scientific experiments with questions/hypothesis/procedure, outlining, and research projects. For an array of cross-curricular interactive writing suggestions, you might want to read *Interactive Writing and Interactive Editing* by Schwartz, Klein, and Shook (2001).

The following photograph of an interactive writing experience in McMinnville, Oregon was taken by Kathy Baird, Reading Recovery Teacher leader. Michelle Khatewoda, the first-grade teacher in whose class the photo was taken, describes her process.

Interactive Writing

Michelle Khatewoda

We started by reading lots of books about plants to build content knowledge. These books were experienced as read alouds, as shared reading experiences, and in guided reading.

I planned for an array of interactive writing sessions to support recall of the information and provide experiences in making word webs and lists.

FIGURE 17.4 This is Darien reading from his book box of familiar favorites. You can see the web on plants we created using interactive writing.

The purpose of the first session was to list what plants need to grow. The purpose of the second session was to list the parts of a plant. After these two lists were written, we discussed what visuals we needed to support our writing. With help from me, they decided the lists would form the foundation for a bulletin board showing what we learned about plants. We painted visuals, used words from the interactive writing, and arranged them on a bulletin board as in the following photo.

FIGURE 17.5 The bulletin board is the showcase for the students' knowledge on plants after an intense study.

Our final interactive writing session focused on constructing a title for our bulletin board. The students could not agree on a single title, so we ended up with two.

After everything was finished and displayed, I explained to the students that this board was for them to use during our plant study to help with writing and other projects we would be doing. They loved reading it during "read the room" and other reading times.

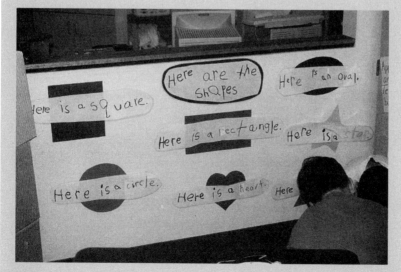

FIGURE 17.6 We do this board the first week of school. I want the students to have it as a reference, as well as learn a few sight words early in the year.

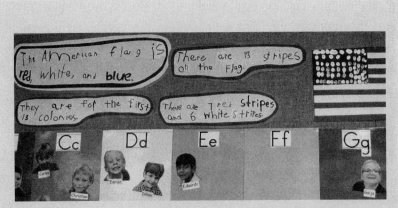

FIGURE 17.7 We did this writing the week after the September 11 attacks. We had been learning the pledge and I felt that the students should know more about the flag so we studied the parts of the flag.

18

. . . .

Guided Writing with Nonfiction

Guided writing, like guided reading, is a small group time when flexible groups meet with a teacher for guidance and support. Because of the small group size, the lesson is far more intense than a whole class lesson. Learners pay close attention and have more opportunity to speak and receive personalized support.

Bring the Craft of Writing into Focus

During guided writing, the teacher can provide link-ups to minilessons shared with the whole class and give an opportunity for the writers to engage with the minilesson concepts while the teacher is close by to guide and support. This small group time might be an opportunity to stretch and expand the writing skills of gifted students, to reteach key writing skills for struggling students, or to demonstrate an informational text feature a group of students would find helpful in their content writing. As in guided reading, this time is built upon learner needs. Groups are small, flexible, and short-term.

Parallels to Guided Reading

I see many parallels between guided reading and guided writing. Both are conducted in a small group setting and emphasize strategies. Both emphasize explicit teaching followed by students independently applying and reflecting upon the strategies that were taught.

Guided Writing as an Extension of Guided Reading

Guided writing can serve as an extension of a guided reading lesson, taking students into the world of the writer in response to their reading. In this case, I ask the students to revisit their guided reading selection to think with the eyes of an informational author. What do we notice about this author's word choice, use of bullets in a list, use of captions, or conventions such as boldface headings? How did these help us as readers? How might we use those tools in our own informational writing?

The next step is to either initiate a new piece of writing to utilize the understandings being shared or to get out writing folders and have the students examine a piece of their informational text. The goal in revisiting writing samples is to consider adding text features that will strengthen their message and offer better support to their readers.

In this scenario, guided writing may be slipped into the time allocated for guided reading with students shifting between guided reading and guided writing. This requires no adjustments in daily schedules as guided writing occurs during an already scheduled time block.

Guided Writing Within Writers Workshop

Guided writing can offer instructional power during Writers Workshop. If you look at your Writers Workshop schedule, you might be able to allocate ten minutes of each workshop for one guided reading group to meet each day. These guided writing groups could be linking up to a whole class minilesson or offering an advanced lesson on voice in informational text. Like guided reading, the goal is to observe learners closely and then match instruction to need while you are close by to provide intense and personal support.

Guided Writing in Content Area Studies

Math, science, social studies, and health all offer rich opportunities to gather small guided writing groups for explicit instruction and support on writing in the content areas. Even a brief session can heighten learner awareness and bring increased skill to their content area writing.

The following guided writing lessons are kernels of possibility to encourage your thinking about strategies and topics for guiding the writers in your life.

Using Models for Writing

Engage a small group in an exploration of a variety of informational texts that have been preselected to represent a variety of ways information can be presented visually. Encourage the students to look for captions, graphs, charts, diagrams, flow charts, tables, and so on. As they browse and observe, engage them in creating a list of text features they notice in the informational texts. Guide a conversation about which text features best suit which purposes. Why might the authors have made the choices they did? A chart such as the following could then be created that lists the features down one side and gives purposes on the other.

Features	Purposes
Caption	Add information about the picture
Graph	Compare information
Flow chart	Show a process

The students could then decide which text features they might use to create a piece of writing based upon a current science, social studies, or math theme. This writing could be done as an interactive writing or personal writing.

Informational Text Planning Sheet

Name _____

My topic is _____

The main idea I hope to convey is:

_____

_____

Major themes:

_____

_____

Supporting details:

_____

_____

My resource(s) for the information include:

_____

_____

_____

Conclusions I hope my readers can draw from this material:

_____

_____

_____

Inviting the Reader into Your Writing

One of the greatest challenges faced by many young writers of informational texts is trying to avoid lists in their writing. As isolated facts are gathered and turned into narrative, the writing often sounds like dictionaries or encyclopedias.

During guided writing, I invite writers to take the role of the animal they are writing about and write as though that animal was talking to the reader. This creates a strong sense of voice that livens up the writing and immediately brings the reader into the conversation.

Writing sample:

Mallard Duck: "I am a mallard drake with jewel tone colors. You should see me in the spring when the emerald feathers on my head are at their most brilliant . . . You'll have to see my white wing patches. When I spread my wings, they shine as white as the snow. From the ground, the white patches blend in with the clouds."

The goals is to write with clarity and voice, incorporating clear descriptions, and language that makes the reader feel involved.

The following are some stems to try:

Please notice that . . .
You'll have to see . . .
Did I mention that . . .
Look at my . . .

Steps to Success with Informational Text Writing

Writer _____ Topic _____ Date _____

In my informational writing, I remembered to include:

A title

Headings

Illustrations

Captions

Drawings with labels

A labeled diagram

A chart

Other

_____

_____

_____

Same Topic/Different Forms of Informational Texts

It can be really interesting to create guided writing groups that are organized by interest, by a particular kind of informational writing in which practice is needed, or to highlight how different forms of informational writing can change the tone of a piece.

I assign each guided writing group a kind of informational text such as persuasive, descriptive, comparison, or time order and explain that it is their job to show what they have learned about a current unit of study using their assigned text structure. They can have one shared piece of writing or produce a book in which individuals contribute pages, but all piece from their team must utilize the assigned structure.

This experience is dependent upon my previous minilessons and guided writing lessons in which I explicitly taught the structures.

Team Writing Experience

Our topic _____

The informational structure is _____

(description, problem/solution, time/order, comparison, cause/effect, narrative)

Team members _____

Make a list of the attributes of your assigned text structure.

What are the essential attributes of _____?

_____

_____

Find an example of this structure and doublecheck your list._____

_____

How will you present your topic using your assigned structure?_____

_____

_____

What role will each group member play in the draft? _____

_____

_____

How will you present your work?_____

_____

_____

What have you learned about writing using the structure of _____?

_____

_____

Leads, Middles, Endings!

Create a classroom resource of powerful information leads, strong middles that keep you going, and endings that summarize. You might develop this as a bulletin board with quotes collected from great informational books, as a Big Book, or in personal logs the students refer to independently.

Encourage the students to include student-authored texts as well as published works in this survey.

Then . . . write:

What makes a good lead? _____

_____

_____

_____

What keeps a reader going in the middle of an informational text?

_____

_____

_____

What are the attributes of a great ending? _____

_____

_____

_____

Writing Tempting Titles

Writer _____ Topic _____ Date _____

Look through some nonfiction books and wonder about the titles. Are they good ones? Poor ones? What makes a title good or bad?

Write five possible titles for the informational writing you are currently developing. Try to make them really interesting. Your job is to write titles that draw in the reader and make the reader want to read what you have written.

1. _____

2. _____

3. _____

4. _____

5. _____

Read your titles to the guided writing group.

Which ones did they like best? Why?

_____

_____

_____

Do your titles suggest different things about your writing? Do they sound interesting?

_____

_____

Represent It!

Guide your students in looking at a life cycle or process. As they learn, encourage them to represent what they are learning in the form of a flow chart or series of illustrations that make the steps clear.

After they illustrate, have them tell what they have learned. Lastly, have them write. This rehearsal of information through illustration and conversation solidifies the content learning and builds energy for writing.

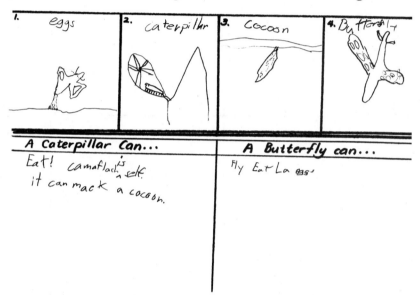

FIGURE 18.1 This sample shows the close ties between student's illustrations, writing, and time-order relationships.

As students gain proficiency, add more steps and boxes. They sketch and write as they read, then use their sketch frames to support their writing.

Sketch Frames for *Represent It!*

Sentence Combining

Sentence combining activities are powerful tools for enhancing content understanding and expanding writing proficiency. To engage in this guided writing lesson, I write short sentences related to a current unit of study on sentence strips, then ask the guided writing group to combine the sentences so that they are more interesting. They cut the words apart, scramble the sentences into lengthier combinations, and add more words and punctuation as needed. There is a great deal of dialogue and often a return to model texts to look at examples of lengthier sentences.

ORIGINAL SENTENCES

> The egg sat on a leaf.
> It was in the sun.
> The egg hatched.
> There was a caterpillar.
> The caterpillar had yellow and black stripes.
> The caterpillar was fuzzy.

COMBINED SENTENCE

The egg, resting on its warm, sunny leaf, hatched into a fuzzy caterpillar with yellow and black stripes.

Reflection

What did we learn? How could we use this as writers of informational text? Why is the longer sentence better? What makes it interesting to a reader?

Follow Up

I usually close the lesson with a direction to the students to return to an informational piece in their writing folder and select some sentences to combine independently.

One of the best follow-ups is to have students check on sentence length. Help them remember:

> Short, short, long
> Long, short, long
> Never short, short, short!

Writing Directions

Precede this guided writing lesson with guided reading of directional resources such as recipes, how-to books, and so on.

Guide the students in making a list of criteria for directions such as:

- Lists materials or ingredients
- Has steps to follow
- The writing sounds bossy

Then, have students attempt to apply the structure to something they know how to do. After their writing is complete, revised, and edited, I always ask them to have someone test their directions by following them exactly as they are written and then giving feedback. This is a wonderful and authentic source of response that almost always results in revisions.

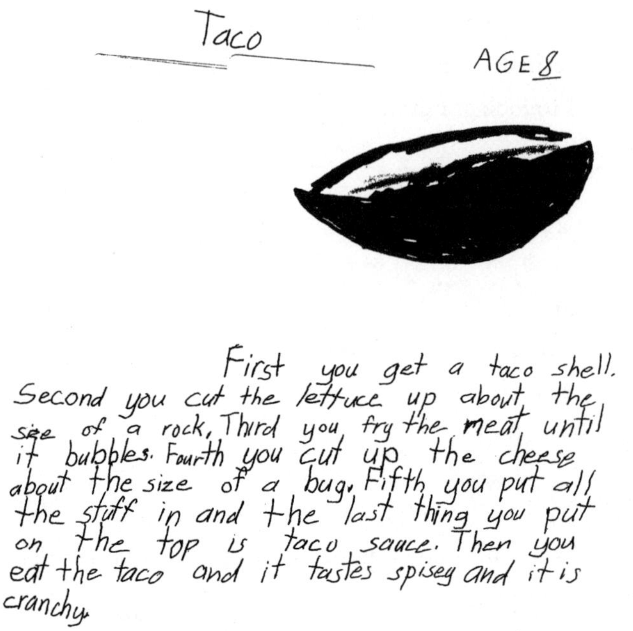

Taco   AGE 8

First you get a taco shell. Second you cut the lettuce up about the size of a rock. Third you fry the meat until it bubbles. Fourth you cut up the cheese about the size of a bug. Fifth you put all the stuff in and the last thing you put on the top is taco sauce. Then you eat the taco and it tastes spisey and it is cranchy.

FIGURE 18.2 An example of a student's written directions.

Writing Directions

Name _____ Date _____

Directions for _____

Materials/ingredients needed _____

The steps to follow:

I asked _____ to test my directions. The feedback I received included:

Parts of my directions that were really good	Revisions I need to make

Writing Sample Test Questions

In an era of high-stakes testing, it is important for students to understand the genre of testing and the nature of the questions that are designed to measure understanding. I often address this by conducting a guided reading lesson with a sample informational text passage. In a small guided reading group, we can really look at the questions, notice the wording, and wonder about strategies such as elimination, identifying distracters, and puzzle together about the structure of the question.

Once the students begin to understand the structure of questions and formats such as: *Which of the following is NOT true?*, we are ready to begin writing our own test questions.

The following questions were written as a follow-up to a guided reading session with a book on wolves. The students worked in partners to craft their "test" questions about the book, then came back together to answer the questions that had been created.

The benefits of writing test questions are many. First, students learn the content. Then they reflect, summarize, and think about what they learned. They learn about questioning and the unique structure of test questions. They also have fun! Trying to trick their friends can be really entertaining!

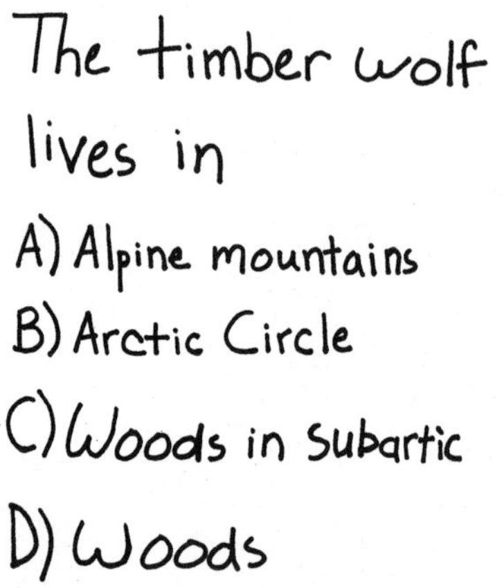

The timber wolf lives in
A) Alpine mountains
B) Arctic Circle
C) Woods in Subartic
D) Woods

FIGURE 18.3 An example of a test question written by two students. Notice how the format includes one correct answer and three distracters just as in a standardized test.

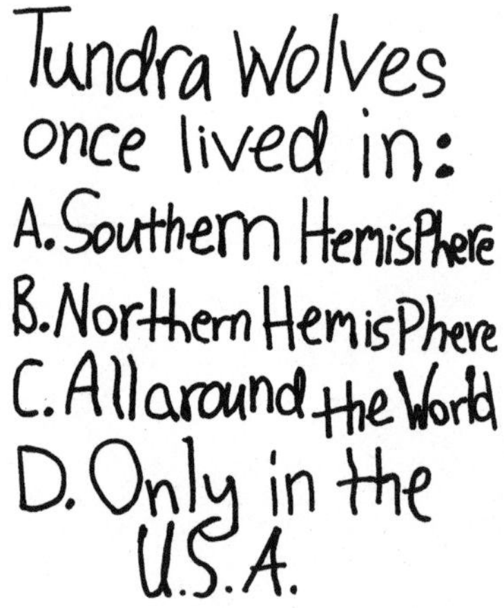

Tundra Wolves once lived in:
A. Southern Hemisphere
B. Northern Hemisphere
C. All around the World
D. Only in the U.S.A.

FIGURE 18.4 Test questions can be written as a follow-up to guided reading or a unit of study.

Creating a Picture Glossary

The small group format of guided writing is perfect for working on non-fiction text features such as an index and glossary. After a guided reading session or during a unit of study, I often gather a guided reading group to create a picture glossary to reflect what we are learning.

ANTS

> Ants are insects and they have three main body parts. They have a head, thorax and abdomen. They also Have antennae which are used for communicating with Other ants and for smelling.

FIGURE 18.5 A student-made picture glossary.

Writing Riddles

Riddles can assist in reflection on a unit of study in the same way that developing questions supports understanding. The structure of riddles with their question/answer format encourages creative thinking and retelling of content. Some possibilities include:

> I fly long distances even though I weigh less than a penny. I have a long pointed beak and like brightly colored flowers. What am I?

> I have spots on my back and two wings shaped like fans. I started out as a caterpillar. What am I?

> I hunt to feed my children until they are one year old. I live in the middle of Africa. I have two colors on my fur, yellow and black. I am an unusual cat and can run 70 miles an hour. What am I?

Compare/Contrast

Lead a guided reading group in gathering information on topics that invite comparison. They might read selections on baboons and monkeys;

alligators and crocodiles; Iroquois and Cheyenne Indians; fir trees and pine trees, and so on. As students gather data, have them list descriptors on strips of paper or three by five cards then place the strips into a Venn diagram showing features that are alike and different.

Create a list of signal words that are often noticed in comparison writing such as *alike, different, in comparison, in contrast to,* and so on. Use the signal words and the descriptions to draft comparison pieces.

Engage your guided writing group with comparison drawings. Comparisons of time, weight, length, distance, and size help readers to make meaning. A scale drawing showing a human swimming next to a whale tells a great deal about the size of the whale. Comparisons help readers to link the known to the unknown.

Opening a Paragraph with a Question

Informational writing often features questions as headings for paragraphs. Survey an array of texts to find several that use questions as headings. Discuss how the questions may help a reader and the role they play in helping a writer to maintain focus.

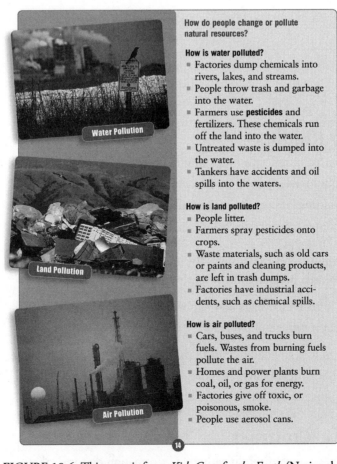

How do people change or pollute natural resources?

How is water polluted?
- Factories dump chemicals into rivers, lakes, and streams.
- People throw trash and garbage into the water.
- Farmers use **pesticides** and fertilizers. These chemicals run off the land into the water.
- Untreated waste is dumped into the water.
- Tankers have accidents and oil spills into the waters.

How is land polluted?
- People litter.
- Farmers spray pesticides onto crops.
- Waste materials, such as old cars or paints and cleaning products, are left in trash dumps.
- Factories have industrial accidents, such as chemical spills.

How is air polluted?
- Cars, buses, and trucks burn fuels. Wastes from burning fuels pollute the air.
- Homes and power plants burn coal, oil, or gas for energy.
- Factories give off toxic, or poisonous, smoke.
- People use aerosol cans.

FIGURE 18.6 This page is from *Kids Care for the Earth* (National Geographic, 2002).

Using Questions to Organize My Writing

Writer _____ Topic _____

Resources used _____

Think of four major questions related to your topic. As you research, gather answers to the questions under each one. Then, convert your list of questions into a narrative on your topic.

Question #1: _____

Possible answers:

_____

Question #2: _____

Possible answers:

_____

Question #3: _____

Possible answers:

_____

Question #4: _____

Possible answers:

_____

Written Narrative
(use more pages if necessary)

Using an Alphabox as a Research Tool

Alphaboxes (Hoyt 1999) are a helpful tool for organizing important ideas from a text or on a topic. A simple grid, such as the one that follows, can be provided for students to use before, during, and after reading.

Before reading, students can insert words reflecting prior knowledge on a topic. During reading, they can record words and phrases they believe are important to the study.

After reading, they can add points they consider to be important or words that reflect their inferences and conclusions related to the reading.

FIGURE 18.7 Using an alphabox to organize my thinking.

The following alphaboxes on Abraham Lincoln and George Washington were used by Kim Bimler at St. John's Lutheran School in Elgin, Illinois as a prewriting organizer for her third graders.

Alphaboxes

George Washington

The reader(s) _____

A	B	C	D
army address Augustine Articles of Confederation American Administration	books brother biographies bullets brilliance brave Boston Tea Party	cabinet chop Cherries Chief Constitutional Convention Colonial courage character Countryman	diaries died daughter determination devotion
E English Executive Mansion Education expedition	**F** father first fables faults frontiers fish Ferry Farm Feb. 22, 1732	**G** George gentleman general	**H** horses hunt hard-working
I Indian fighter Independence Inauguration Day	**J** Journals Jacky	**K**	**L** letters loyal landscape leadership lieutenant
M Mount Vernon Martha Major maps married military manners	**N** New England	**O** officer observant	**P** President pioneer plantation Patsy Public
Q questions	**R** reports read retirement revolution religion	**S** Surveyor Scout school Sisters supplies Smallpox Service Stamp Act	**T** tree troops treaty
U United States Union	**V** Virginia Valley	**W** War Weaknesses Wilderness Whiskey Rebellion	**XYZ** Youth Yorktown

FIGURE 18.8

Alphaboxes

Abraham Lincoln

The reader(s) _____

A	B	C	D
Abe ax American assassinated Abraham armies April 15, 1865	book battle born Booth	coffin college Civil War cabin court campaign Constitution Commander country court candidate	died Douglas Dec. of Indep. democracy debate Democrat
E educated Eddie Emancipation election	**F** Feb. 12, 1809 Frederick farming fields freedom fence flag frontier	**G** Gettysburg government	**H** honest horse House of Representatives heroic
I Illinois Indiana Inaugural Address	**J** John joker	**K** Kentucky	**L** Lincoln log legislature law exams lawyer
M married morning milk sickness	**N** Nancy North New Salem Negroes	**O** ox office	**P** President 16th Proclamation plow pioneer politics play peace pistol postmaster
Q questioning	**R** Robert rails Rail Splitter raid	**S** Sarah shot soldier school slavery speech Springfield sons surveyor stories South Supreme	**T** Ted turkey train trade Thomas theatre
U unspeakable union United States understanding	**V** volunteers	**W** Willie Washington DC War Whigs White House weep World	**XYZ** young Youth

FIGURE 18.9

Third graders created these alphaboxes then incorporated their research into their writing.

Alphaboxes

The topic _____

The reader(s) _____

A	B	C	D
E	F	G	H
I	J	K	L
M	N	O	P
Q	R	S	T
U	V	W	XYZ

Guided Writing Self-Assessment: Primary

Writer _____

Topic _____ Date _____

❑ My illustration has details about my topic.

❑ I included labels in my drawing.

❑ My writing explains what is in my illustration.

❑ I re-read to make sure I had made sense.

❑ I placed a title above my writing or my illustration.

❑ I inserted a caption near the illustration.

❑ I left spaces between my words.

❑ There are periods at the ends of my sentences.

❑ There is a capital at the beginning of each sentence.

❑ I checked for words that might need spelling help.

❑ My opening is interesting to a reader.

❑ I combined short sentences to make them more interesting.

Guided Writing Self-Assessment: Intermediate

Writer _____

Topic _____ Date _____

The Organization of My Writing

❑ Information is organized around topics.

❑ There are headings to help the reader.

❑ There is an interesting beginning.

❑ The end summarizes key ideas.

❑ There are topic sentences.

❑ A reader could identify a key word or phrase for each paragraph.

Visual Supports

I provided the following visuals to support my information

_____

❑ The page(s) are organized so that visuals and text appear in interesting configurations.

❑ There is a table of contents, index, glossary, captions, and/or

_____

❑ I have shared my writing with others to check the clarity of the content.

❑ I have edited my work.

❑ While writing this piece, I learned _____ about the craft of writing informational texts. Use additional pages if necessary to reflect on what you learned.

Reflecting on Informational Experiences with Poetry

Poetry brings joy, causes reflection, invites inferences, and helps make connections in our thinking. When children have opportunities to use poetry and poetic language to show what they have learned, many find that they can use their personal strengths to reach greater levels of understanding. There are many nonfiction poems to share with your students.

Using Visualization to Write Informational Poetry

Ask students to close their eyes and visualize themselves immersed and truly living the topic they have been studying . . . they might imagine themselves as a pioneer trying to steer a wagon over a rocky, treacherous road or pulling frightened animals and a floating, tipsy wagon across a raging river. They might imagine themselves immersed in the world of the whale, deep under the sea with their huge whale family pushing through the waters around them, calves close to their sides.

To turn visualization into poetry, I ask students to use their senses to describe their visualizations. What do you see? Look to your right, your left, above you. What do you hear? Do you hear the pinging of the whales singing to each other, the mewing of the whale calf, or the great blast of air as a baleen whale surfaces?

As students use their senses to take their visualization into a highly personal space, I ask them to jot down words and phrases, not sentences, that describe what they see, hear, feel, taste, smell, and so on.

This results in a rich word cache from which the poetry can flow.

SAMPLE: BALEEN WHALES

I *see*:
Deep blue ocean
Surging bodies pushing through the water
Baleen exposed as krill are sifted
Calves, nudging close, venturing away
A rush of force as the whale surfaces for air
The darting of smaller beings moving from the path

I *hear*:
Expulsion of air
Slap of a huge tail
Friendly pings

I *feel*:
Awe
Respect
Appreciation
Puzzlement at their treatment in the past

As you can see, even the listing of phrases for each sense has a strong poetic feel. Students can treat their lists as poems in and of themselves or merge senses to create other kinds of poetic formats.

Informational Poetry

Writer _____

Topic _____ Date _____

Try to immerse yourself into the world you are studying. Close your eyes and truly visualize yourself right in the middle of the action. What do you see? What do you hear? What are you feeling? If you reached out to touch something, what would it be? What would it feel like? Are there any smells associated with this visualization? Is there anything you could taste?

List words and phrases that describe your visualization and your understanding of the topic.

I SEE	I HEAR	I FEEL
_____	_____	_____
_____	_____	_____
_____	_____	_____
_____	_____	_____

WHEN I REACH OUT AND TOUCH, THE TEXTURES ARE	I SMELL	I TASTE
_____	_____	_____
_____	_____	_____
_____	_____	_____
_____	_____	_____

Share your lists with a partner. Ask your partner to try to visualize with you as you read your words and phrases.

List Poems

First graders, after blowing bubbles and preparing to read a guided reading selection on bubbles, write:

> Bubbles
>
> Round bubbles
>
> Floating bubbles
>
> Bubbles in a group
>
> Soapy bubbles
>
> Stretching bubbles
>
> Pop! They are gone.

Kindergarten students, after dipping their feet in paint and creating a mural, write:

> Foot painting
>
> Tiptoe
>
> Splat
>
> Splatter
>
> Squishing between our toes
>
> Paint!

Fifth graders, after dissecting owl pellets, write:

> Owl pellets
>
> Bones
>
> Hair
>
> A tiny skull
>
> Understanding a hunter

In Hood River, Oregon first graders experiencing the joys of freshly picked Hood River apples write:

> Apples, Apples, Apples
>
> Crunchy, crispy, curvy, caramel apples.
>
> Mushy, munchy, mucky, monster apples.
>
> Yummy, yucky, yellow, young apples.
>
> Wormy, wonderful, wet, washed apples.
>
> Good, golden, great, green apples.
>
> Red, rotten, round, ripe apples.
>
> Smooth, smelly, sparkly, shiny apples.
>
> Juicy, giant, junky, jumbo apples.
>
> Hard, holey, handy, humongous apples.
>
> Apples, apples, apples!
>
> —by Phyliss Coats' first-grade class

Diane Walworth, Heinemann Consultant for First Steps USA, guided first and second graders in writing:

Leaves
Lovely, little, light leaves
Beautiful, brown, big leaves
Wet, windy, wonderful leaves
Crunchy, colorful, crooked leaves
Nasty, nice, nutty leaves
Falling, fun, funny leaves
Gliding, good, green leaves
Cracked, crispy, crushed leaves
Pretty piles of pinkish leaves
Leaves, Leaves, Leaves

19

....

Research Strategies

We all do research. We check out advertisements for the best price on products we need or want. We survey recipe books to find a recipe that best matches our mood, our taste buds, or ingredients we have on hand. We talk to our friends to learn their opinions on topics of interest, or check out the *T.V. Guide* to research programs that are available at a given time. As we bring children into the world of research, I believe one of the best things we can do is make research a part of daily classroom life, just as it is part of daily living. When research is placed on a pedestal and saved for that big research project at the end of the year, it suddenly sounds hard. It sounds like something you do for a grade rather than something for yourself.

The following strategies are some teasers to get you started weaving research into the daily fabric of your classroom. Find your personal passions. Explore them publicly. Let the children see your enthusiasm and your research strategies (Harvey 1998). Write with them to share what you are learning and place your name in the table of contents next to the piece of research you contribute to class research efforts. Instead of research, you may want to call it "We Search."

A first stop on the research trail . . . adults in your school and community. They all have passions and interests that can be explored and researched. Once you have established a culture of research, you can easily move from interviewing adults to interviewing and learning from the experts in your classroom. This primary source research is important to all researchers. Teaching children to value interviews as research will empower them to contact "experts" personally and not allow their future research efforts to become limited by what they can find in books.

Experts in Our Community

Name	Area(s) of Expertise	Job
Mrs. Hoyt	Snow skiing	Writer
	Water skiing	Mom
	Reading	Teacher
	Gardening	
	Walking dogs	
	Making appetizers	
Mr. Hoyt	Snow skiing	Sales Rep
	Water skiing	Dad
	Fishing	
	Duck hunting	
	Elk hunting	
	Dog training	
	Newspaper reading	
	Barbequing	

Experts in Our School

Name	Area(s) of Expertise	Job
Mr. Martin	Woodworking	School
	Fixing cars	Custodian
	Building clocks	
Mrs. Aloya	Knitting	School
	Flower gardening	Secretary
	Bird watching	

Experts in Our Classroom

Name	Area(s) of Expertise
Juan	Skateboarding
	Soccer
Eli	Beads
	Horses
Marta	Swimming

Primary Research Formats

Children need to know that we do research every day. We do research at the grocery store when we read prices and select the best value for our money. To make research approachable and fun, we can draw upon the 1980s *Math Their Way* approach to graphing and data gathering.

Researching and Building a Bar Graph

Have students look at their shoes and then line up according to the kind of shoe they are wearing today. Everyone with sneakers in one line, boots in another, sandals in a third. Or, line up according to who has laces, buckles, or slip ons. This kind of research is developmentally very approachable to young children and can be easily presented in the form of a graph.

The information you gather can be organized as a bar graph. When you add a written text explaining the research you conducted, you have a complete research study, language lesson, and math exploration all in one.

Researchers could branch out around the school to interview adults to learn: Who has a pet? Who likes to garden? How do you get to school?

Research Question of the Day

Many teachers like to post a daily research question. As students enter the classroom, they respond to the research question by placing a clothespin with their name on it next to their answer to the question.

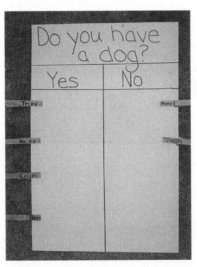

FIGURE 19.1 Students respond to a daily research question such as this.

This process works best for questions with Yes/No responses such as "Do you have a dog?" "Do you ride a bike?" "Is your hair brown?" "Do you like marshmallows?" Emergent students can be supported by adding a picture next to the question.

Daily research questions are a great way to check attendance as a quick glimpse at the chart makes it clear if any clothespins remain unused that day.

Students can easily take this to independence by generating their own questions and then conducting interviews asking those interviewed to sign their names on the side of the chart that tells their answer. See the following example.

INTERVIEW QUESTION

Do you like spinach?

Yes	No
Alan	Samantha
Sergio	Martine
	Brandon
	Kyle

In this research format, students write their own names, which is great practice for name writing.

SOME OTHER POSSIBILITIES:

What do you know about nonfiction?

> It's true (Shannon)
> You learn things (Juan)
> You learn more about what you already know (Alan)

Things that are . . .

Living	Not Living

INTERVIEWING ADULTS

> Ask: *What nonfiction sources do you read? Why?*
> Report back to the class

Researching Through Experience

As we attempt to create a culture of research, it is helpful to use the word *research* whenever you can. When you conduct science experiences with worms, blow bubbles, collect rainwater, or create an underwater garden, you are researching. When you take math manipulatives and attempt to solve a problem, you are researching. When you weigh garbage in the cafeteria during a recycling unit, you are researching. As you read aloud on topics of interest to the class, you are researching. The teaching day is laden with real experiences and real opportunities to research!

We can label our observations as research. The following research writing about Smug, the hamster, is based on observations and descriptions of real life in caring for a pet.

FIGURE 19.2

FIGURE 19.3

FIGURE 19.4 These photographs and the writing show research-based writing.

Research Workshop

Some teachers like to establish a Research Workshop. This may be an ongoing effort or a unit that appears periodically in your schedule. The idea of a Research Workshop is to have everyone researching! The research could be anything from interviewing (as described earlier) to reading and writing on topics of personal interest.

Within the workshop, you create a culture of conversation about research. Just as in writers workshop, you open with a research minilesson and close with a sharing session. During the workshop, students might work in teams to conduct team research or gather in small groups to share individual research efforts. Within their teams, they discuss research topics/strategies just as we do in writers workshop.

RESEARCH GROUP GUIDELINES

Meet daily.

Tell what you are learning.

Share your resources.

Explain your challenges.

What are you finding to be interesting?

Ask questions after each person shares.

FIGURE 19.5 By narrowing the range of research topics, I have fewer resources to gather and can provide highly explicit demonstrations of the processes in data collection and synthesis for writing.

Narrowing Choices While Learning the Steps

Because passion and interest are so crucial to research, I try to always ensure that students have some measure of choice in their research, but the choices don't always have to be wide open.

When students are first learning to be researchers, a narrower range of choices best supports the learning process. When the range of options is narrowed to one particular style of writing or data gathering, I can explicitly model strategies and procedures for students to emulate. I can provide team research opportunities where they have the support of partners as they research and write. While teaching the procedures of personal research and doing lots of demonstrations, students might all be studying a topic such as Westward Migration or Life Cycles. The range is narrowed so that I can make sure that resources are available and that strategies are clearly taught. Once the research strategies are learned, the door can open to the wide world of personal research.

With explicit modeling of gathering of resources, data collection, team research, and writing, students begin to load their tool kits with research strategies and build toward independence as researchers. During this time, I can spend my time planning high-quality demonstrations because I have narrowed the range of resources that need to be gathered.

Research Plan

Researcher _____ Topic _____

My big questions: What do I most want to learn?

- _____

- _____

- _____

- _____

How will I find answers? What sources are likely to help? Be sure to include at least one interview related to your topic. _____

_____

Interview

Written Sources

Source   Author   Publisher

_____   _____   _____

_____   _____   _____

_____   _____   _____

Data-Gathering Strategy
There are many ways to gather data. You can take notes, cut them up, and classify them; use index cards or graphic organizers; combine sketching and writing; or ?

To gather my information, I will _____

How will you present what you have learned? (Write a report, make an oral presentation, create a book, make a poster, or _____)

Planning Checklists

Name _____

Research Topic _____ Date _____

Preresearch Checklist
I have:

- [ ] Chosen my topic
- [ ] Selected my resources, including at least one interview
- [ ] Made a data-gathering plan
- [ ] Identified how I will present my research

Postresearch Checklist
My final product:

- [ ] Is written in my own words. I did not copy from books.
- [ ] Includes visuals to support my audience
- [ ] Contains big ideas on the topic as well as details
- [ ] Includes clear descriptions to support visualizations
- [ ] Has clearly organized sections
- [ ] Has an introduction and a conclusion

Ali Taylor is a second-grade teacher at Columbus Elementary in McMinnville, Oregon whose students live in a culture of research. They research topics of interest as well as the forms of informational writing that best help us to express our information. Ali describes a process of researching procedures students know how to do and then writing how-to manuals on their topics.

Researching and Showing What We Know

Writing Directions and How-To Manuals

Ali Taylor

My approach to research and writing how-to manuals has been more successful than in previous years because I gathered a collection of books and resources that show how to do things. I collected how-to manuals, directions from food packages, recipe books, manuals, directions to games, DVD players, and so on. We examined these different sources and listed their attributes. We found that these sources listed steps in a process, often included a materials list, and had very directive language. Some had illustrations to support the steps while others had photographs and illustrations of a finished product.

A fun way to initiate the research and how-to writing is to have the children write instructions for making a peanut butter and jelly sandwich. I then use their instructions to actually make a sandwich, following the steps in their writing exactly, while the students observe. There will be much hilarity when you set the peanut butter jar on top of the loaf of bread, or you scoop peanut butter out of the jar with your fingers because they forgot to tell you to use a knife or to take the bread out of the packaging. Children quickly learn how important it is to think through every step when writing how-to pieces.

The Steps

1. Research What You Know: Ask them to talk with another student for 1 minute about some of the things that they could teach people to do . . . feeding a pet, creating an art project, fixing a skateboard, babysitting, or cooking.

2. Set Up the Directions: Show the children how to fold a large piece of white paper into eighths and model for them how they will write their title in the first square ("How to . . ."). The second square will show illustrations and words for the materials and ingredients they will need, and then subsequent squares

would be labeled Step 1, Step 2, etc. The final frame should show an illustration of the finished project or recipe and have an interesting ending sentence to tie the writing back to the title.

3. I remind them that this is research. They are telling about something they already understand, but they need to be accurate and use sources to ensure they have included all needed steps.

How to Make a
Fruit cake

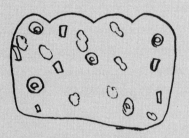

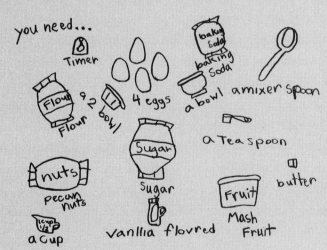

FIGURE 19.6 Students write and illustrate how-to manuals.

20

Investigations
These Are So Cool!

My introduction to Investigations came from Patty Jo Foley, a dedicated teacher in Beaverton, Oregon who gleaned the idea while visiting schools in Australia. I was excited by the emphasis Investigations placed on student research combined with a clear understanding of the importance of visuals in informational text. I have worked on Investigations with students from kindergarten through middle school and found great success at all levels. I first wrote about Investigations in *Revisit, Reflect, Retell* (Hoyt 1999) but have continued to refine my understanding of this powerful tool. The more I have explored Investigations with learners, the more convinced I have become of their power for synthesizing learning and teaching the craft of informational writing.

FIGURE 20.1

FIGURE 20.2

These Investigations show the detail and information students weave naturally into their work.

The core components of an Investigation include:

- a double-page layout. Imagine opening an informational text and seeing both pages treated as one visual image; the fold line in the center is ignored.
- a brief investigation of a topic. Different than a report, an investigation is supposed to be a toe dip into the topic . . . a *brief* exploration.
- a conscious effort to use the features of informational texts such as captions, titles, boldface headings, charts, close-ups, cross-sections, diagrams, and so on. (I have always encouraged students to include a minimum of one illustration and one diagram although I find students often add much more than the minimums.)
- concise text that tells essential information on the topic.

Because Investigations are considered published material, students engage in all steps in the writing process, including a prewriting plan that sketches out the plan for their visuals and their text blocks.

Demonstrating an Investigation Through Modeled Writing

I bring in resources of personal interest to me such as a books on dog training, snow skiing, golf, or brochures on a trip I would love to take to Perth, Australia. If I have any personal photos related to my area of interest, I bring those as well. I also bring in a variety of informational texts that make good use of visual space and integrate diagrams, charts, and other text features into an attractive two-page layout. News magazines such as *National Geographic for Kids*, *Time for Kids*, and *Sports Illustrated for Kids* are good examples as are many of the informational Big Books currently on the market. I want the students to understand that this isn't just an activity—we are attempting to integrate into our writing the conventions we associate with informational texts. I explain that my Investigation will be the focus of modeled writing for several days.

Then, I begin to think aloud about creating an Investigation.

STEPS IN THE MODELING/THINK ALOUD PROCESS

1. Selecting a topic. I think out loud about my various choices and then share my process of making a decision. I select skiing for my investigation.

2. Once my topic is chosen, I begin a sketch of what I would like my investigation to look like. I use large paper and make a dotted line down the center to reflect where the fold line will go through the middle. As I sketch, I think out loud about one illustration that would really support what I know about skiing and how the text blocks might work with that illustration. (I decide that a mountain with a chairlift running up the side

and a lodge at the bottom will be my main illustration and I am going to place it in the middle of the page.) I also think aloud about the informational text features that will help me communicate about my topic. Do I want a chart, a graph, a close-up diagram, a map? (I decide on a close-up diagram of the bindings on my skis and a map of where the best ski areas in Oregon are located.) Next, I sketch in where I envision the diagram and map fitting on the page, along with boxes for the title, the text, and captions. I also sketch in a spot where I am going to include a real photograph of me on skis.

3. Now that I have a plan for my investigation, I am ready to start crafting my text and doing any research I think I need. I know a lot in my head about skiing so I first decide what I want to communicate in my Investigation. That is my **main idea**. Next, I decide that my research is going to be on What's New in Ski Equipment. (I take time to add a text box to show where on the page this will go.)

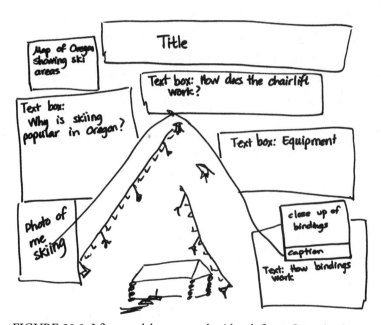

FIGURE 20.3 I first model my own plan/sketch for an Investigation.

4. Now I am ready to research and write. I show students how I look through ski magazines and brochures, getting a lot of information from pictures. Then I take time to jot my thoughts in the form of a note, list of key phrases, or a sketch. I then demonstrate how to turn my notes and sketches into connected narrative for each of the text boxes I have planned on my Investigation.

5. One of the last steps I take before revising and editing is to show students how I cite my sources. I expect all students, even kindergarten and first graders, to be able to write the title of resources they used and the authors into their Investigation. Writers cite their sources and it is never to early to learn how to do so.

6. Ultimately, I produce an edited, brightly colored Investigation that the students now thoroughly understand.

7. Investigations can be saved as single sheets, arranged into classbooks, wall stories, or kept in personal Investigation books. If I am having students keep personal Investigation books, they create their final versions in 8.5 × 11 stapled books. When these are opened, it is easy to access the double-page spread and there is a history over time of the learner's various Investigations. Then, as in well-crafted informational text, I ask them to insert page numbers, a table of contents, index and perhaps even a glossary. When Investigations are used regularly, students can end up with several volumes of Investigation books they have created and a wonderful keepsake of their studies over the course of a year.

8. *Optional:* Interesting topic-related borders can be added to Investigations. An investigation on spiders might have spider webs or spiders sketched all around the perimeter of the page. An investigation on Dalmatian dogs might have spots around the edge, and so on. While these are motivating to the students, I have discovered that some students spend more time on the border than on the research and writing. As a result, the borders have often turned into an option that students are welcome to take home and complete. They are beautiful, but time-consuming.

Investigation Planning Sheet

Name _____ Topic of My Investigation _____

The key points I want to communicate are:

Some facts I want to include:

Text features I will include (title, headings, captions, diagram, chart, close-up, cross-section, photograph, drawing, labels, other _____)

A sketch of my Investigation:

I ❑ will or ❑ will not be including a border.

Selecting Topics

When students are ready to select topics, I always emphasize choice and interest so the motivation of students is very high as we begin an Investigation.

Sometimes I ask students to focus their Investigations on a current unit of study such as "Oceans." In this case, they would all be planning an investigation about the ocean but there would still be room for choice as students could do research on whales, dolphins, deep sea fishing, or any ocean-related topic they found to be of interest.

At other times, I give the students complete free choice as during writers workshop. When the choices are completely open-ended, the Investigations are usually focused on personal areas of interest such as gymnastics, soccer, motorcycles, butterflies, poisonous snakes, or planting seeds in the garden, just as in the Investigation they watched me model in my Investigation on skiing.

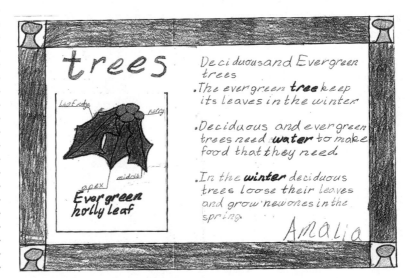

FIGURE 20.4 Amalia grade 2.

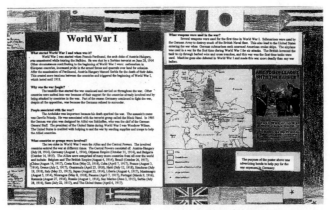

FIGURE 20.5 Grade 6 investigation on World War I.

When to Use Investigations

Investigations can be used in a variety of ways. They can be a guided writing experience with a small group as a part of writers workshop or in response to guided reading. They could be a whole class interaction as part of a unit of study. I know many teachers who have had wonderful success suspending writers workshop for one week a month and engaging the students with Investigations during that time period while others have set aside twenty minutes every day to work on Investigations related to content area study. In these classrooms, students develop Investigations on science, social studies, health, and math concepts.

The Possibilities Are Limitless

Investigations solidify understandings about content, about text structure, and about visual presentations. As I continue to work with Investigations I realize that this is a structure with a long life span. We live in an information age in which we can no longer expect to know everything. What is important is our ability to find the information we need quickly and efficiently, then represent our understandings in ways that are visually appealing and meaningful to others.

Investigations in the Classroom: Making It Personal

The following vignettes about Investigations have been written by classroom teachers who attended seminars in which I shared the Investigation process. Their use of Investigations and the successes of their students are a celebration of the power of the process. I believe the following classroom examples are important as they show the absolute practicality of this process. As you reflect on the following adaptations created by these fine teachers, please consider ways you could make Investigations work with your students and your curriculum. The voices of these teachers show how flexible the process can be and how naturally Investigations can fit into instruction across the grades.

I remember with fondness the day Jodi Wilson first saw my Investigation examples. She was working as a consultant in Beaverton teaching classes and supporting teachers with classroom demonstrations. She became so excited by the format that she borrowed my examples and quickly headed to the local copy center so she would have something concrete to share with teachers and children.

The following Investigation planning sheets and rubrics are designed by Jodi as part of her current work in Spokane, Washington.

Investigation Planning Sheet

Name _____ Date _____

My **topic/title** will be _____

My **border** will look like this (Draw a sample)

[ ]

The type of **visual information** I will include will be:

A **map** with key   OR   A **diagram** with title, caption, and labels

My **written information** will be: ☐ a recount ☐ a summary

Three main ideas I will include are:

_____

_____

_____

This is a sketch showing the layout of my investigation:

[ ]

Planning for My Investigation

Name _____ Date _____

My topic: _____

My map or diagram will look like this:

My drawing will be of:

My border will look like this:

The written information will be organized like this:

By Jodi Wilson and Linda Hoyt. © 2002 by Linda Hoyt from *Make It Real*. Portsmouth, NH: Heinemann.

Investigation Rubric: Self-Assessment

Name _____

Investigation Title _____

Date _____

Text Features	4	3	2	1
Title				
√ Interesting, catchy, exciting				
√ Bold print/color/fancy font				
Written Information				
√ Includes three different ideas				
√ Paraphrased information in own words				
√ Cursive, printed, or typed neatly				
√ Dictionary spelling				
Diagram/Map				
√ Labels/picture captions				
√ Titles or subheadings				

Goal for next investigation:

_____

_____

_____

What score would you give yourself for this investigation? Look at the criteria above and rate yourself on your overall performance.	4	3	2	1

By Jodi Wilson and Linda Hoyt. © 2002 by Linda Hoyt from *Make It Real*. Portsmouth, NH: Heinemann.

Investigation Rubric: Self-Assessment (*continued*)

Resources used (title and author):

1._____

2._____

3._____

4._____

Investigation Rubric

Score	Characteristics
4	√ Title, border, **two types** of written text, map, and diagram with text √ White space completely used √ Extensive use of color and different fonts
3	√ Title, border, written text, map, **and** diagram √ Minimal white space √ Balance of color and pencil work
2	√ Title, border, written text, map, or diagram √ Some white space remains √ Some color and pencil work
1	√ Title, border, written text, map, or diagram

Tom Wrightman is a second-grade teacher at Elk Meadow Elementary in Bend, Oregon. Tom has done presentations all around the United States focused on his literacy program for young readers and writers. After attending a seminar I did in Bend, Tom integrated the Key Word Strategy (see the chapter on deepening understanding) into the Investigation process. The key words became boldface type in the completed investigations.

A Process of Investigation in a Second-Grade Classroom

Tom Wrightman

When a child learns to walk they begin with tiny steps. With continued practice, the steps become larger and are done with more confidence. As practice continues, the walk becomes a run. This learning process is similar to that of a beginning writer learning to put information from a text down in a reportable form. How does a beginning writer learn to take a nonfiction text and extract the important information from it? How does the information come from the page to their written text and become transformed into more than just mere copying of the words?

My goal was to give students a tool for identifying important facts from a text and then putting that information in a reportable form that could be used by other children to learn about a topic. This is just a small step in the larger picture of becoming a proficient writer of reports.

After reading books about owls and visiting the High Desert Museum, which involved a presentation on owls, we were ready to start preparing a way to share what we'd learned. If the students had as little as a key word to start with, that would give them a starting point and focus for their writing.

Step 1

I selected a new piece about owls that was unfamiliar to the students. I showed them a picture from the text and asked them what words the author might use in a story about this picture. I wanted them to become familiar with words that were in the text. I also prompted them with other words in the text, but not listed by the children. After listing the words, we read the text together. We called these words "key words." The list of key words, the picture, and the text were posted on the board. Then I took a post-it note and wrote one of the key words on it. Next, I modeled how to write a sentence with the key word in it. We worked as a whole group writing a number of sentences with different key words. The writing of sentences with key words was modeled in different ways for the next couple of days.

Step 2

I obtained another picture and piece of text about owls. I shared the picture again and repeated the process as in step one. Once I was confident that most kids were familiar with the key words, I paired them up. I handed them a copy of the text to read in pairs. I found it very encouraging that almost all of the children were able to read the piece with very little trouble. We gathered back together and talked about what was learned from the reading. Next, I gave each of them a post-it note and had them find a quiet place to read together again. This time they were to write a key word from the text on the post-it note that they felt was important to the topic. After everyone gathered together, we talked as a group about the key words and why they were selected. Finally, I collected their stories and gave them small sentence strips. Working with their partners again, the children wrote a sentence for the key word they wrote on the post-it notes. The children put their finished sentence on the board after reading them to me.

Owlets are very fluffy. They
have state beaks! And stay
In there nest for 3 months.

FIGURE 20.6 Students write sentences for their key words.

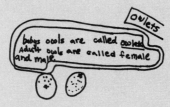

FIGURE 20.7 Another example of key words in sentences.

Step 3

I wanted to reintroduce one of the characteristics of nonfiction text to the children, and selected bold print. After we did this we returned to the sentences written in step two. I asked the children what word they would bold in their sentences . . . the response was their key word! I took one of their sentences and had the child come up and trace over it with a black felt pen. This modeled how to bold a word so it stood out and told the reader that this is an important word.

Our next main focus was to use the key word and the information in their sentence to help us determine what kind of diagram would be appropriate to match their sentence. I used a diagram from a nonfiction text, and showed how it was connected to the text and the topic and how it helped us better understand what the text was telling us. I also pointed out how the diagram used labels to highlight its parts. The children took their sentences, highlighted their key word, and made a first attempt at a diagram that would match the information in their sentence.

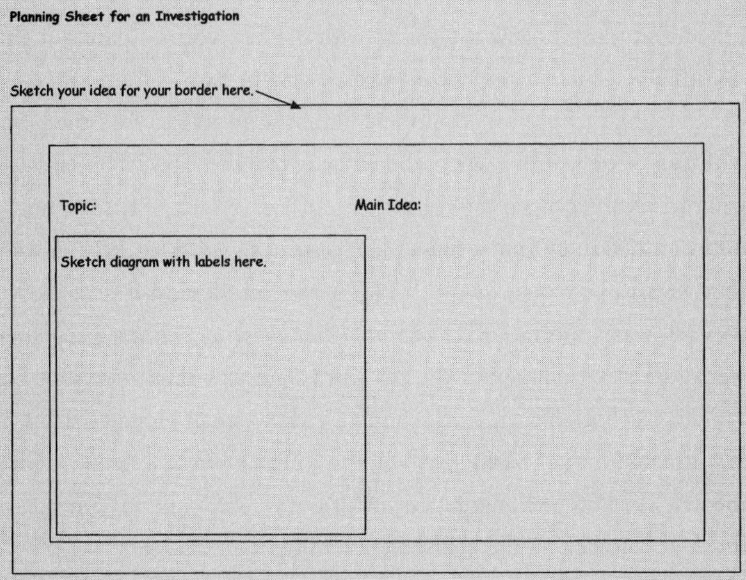

Planning Sheet for an Investigation

Sketch your idea for your border here.

Topic: Main Idea:

Sketch diagram with labels here.

FIGURE 20.8 Text for planning page: planning sheet for an Investigation. Sketch your idea for your border here.

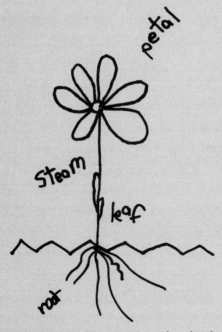

FIGURE 20.9 Topic—Main Idea: sketch a diagram with labels here.

Step 4

It was at this point that the children were ready to attempt their own investigation that encouraged the use of the above skills. We stayed with the topic of owls because of the wealth of information the children now possessed. We decided on researching how owls hunt and baby owls. I collected information on the two main ideas and found pictures to go with each. As a group we created a list of key words for each main idea just by looking at the pictures. Again, I made sure words were included that were in the text. After the list was recorded on the board, I had the children pair up with someone that had the same main idea. This time they were to read the text and talk about the key words they felt were important to learning about this main idea. When that was completed they picked up three post-it notes each and wrote down their three key words from the text. Then they brought the text to me, shared their key words, and took a paper that they could write a sentence with each key word. This became their body of their report.

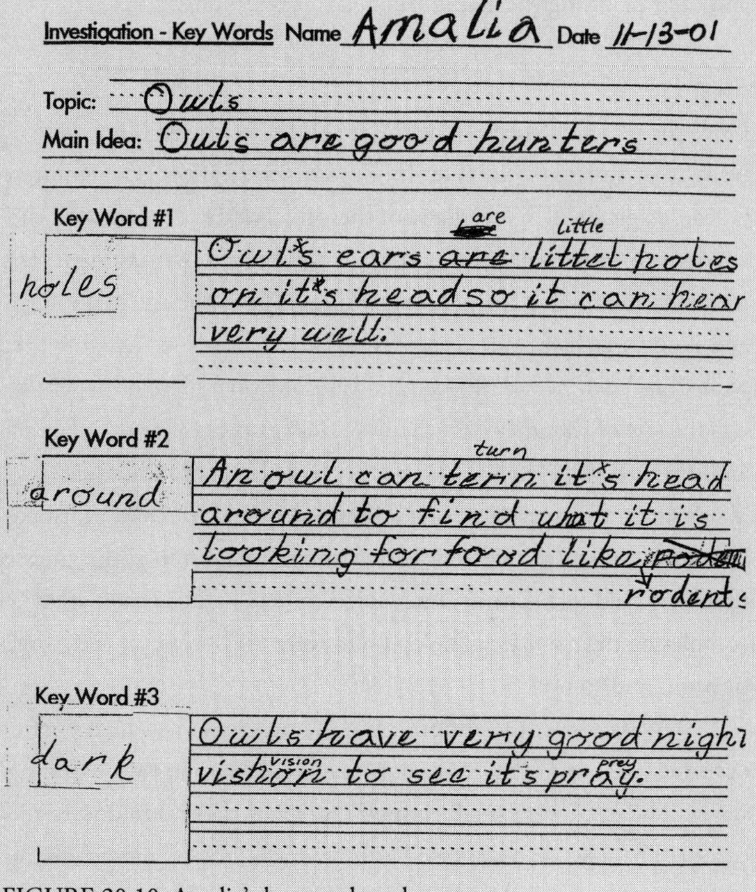

Investigation - Key Words Name **Amalia** Date *11-13-01*

Topic: Owls

Main Idea: Owls are good hunters

Key Word #1

holes

Owl's ears are littel holes (are) (little) on it's head so it can hear very well.

Key Word #2

around

An owl can tern it's head (turn) around to find what it is looking for food like rodent rodents

Key Word #3

dark

Owls have very good night vishon to see it's pray. (vision) (prey)

FIGURE 20.10 Amalia's key words and sentences.

Some children added additional sentences to complement the key word if they wanted to include more information. The act of writing without the text in front of them encouraged the children to access their base of knowledge about owls and put it down in a meaningful way. The key word was then highlighted.

Step 5

The purpose of this step was modeling what their investigation would look like when it was completed. After modifying Linda Hoyt's planning sheet, Revisit, Reflect, Retell (1999) I demonstrated what areas had to be included before they could proceed to the final draft. Keeping in mind the topic and their main idea: owls and hunting, or owls and their babies, they would plan out their border, their diagram (complete with parts labeled), write out the topic, and write out the main idea. The key is making sure the parts are all focused on their topic. I would ask questions like, "If I read your main idea, would the border remind me of it?" Or "Do your facts and your diagram work together to help me understand the information better?" Once this was modeled, the children took their sheet with their sentences on it and their planning sheet and roughed out their ideas.

Step 6

Once the plan and the sentences were complete the children were ready to complete the final draft of their investigation. The children taped "magic lines" to the back of their final draft. This allowed the children to write their information neatly. Prior to writing their sentences on the final draft they were edited. The topic, the main idea, and their three facts were done first. The key words were highlighted with a black felt pen. The diagram was done on a piece of paper that was the size of the square on the final draft paper. Once the diagram and the parts were labeled, the picture was glued into the square. Working on this separate paper allowed the child to make a mistake without ruining the page that had all the writing on it. If they messed up they would just start on a new piece of paper. The final part is completing their border. The children were very proud of their Investigations and so was I.

The success of the children and the process of this investigation occurred because of the small steps that were taken in the beginning stages. The steps were small enough that all of the children were successful. The steps were modeled and practiced many times, allowing confidence to grow.

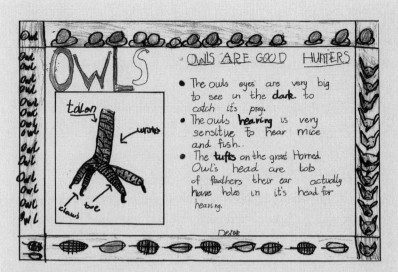

FIGURE 20.11

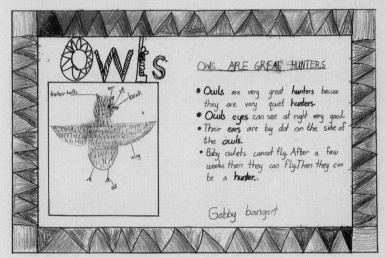

FIGURE 20.12

Two of the Investigations completed by my students. Notice the boldface type reflecting their key words.

Investigations: Teaching Research to Third Graders

Natashya Hays, Third-Grade Teacher, Bend, Oregon

Animals seem to be a topic of interest for almost any third grader I've encountered. Therefore, I thought the topic was a good vehicle through which to teach my third graders about research and how to present that information. I had five main goals with this project:

- For my students to be able to collect data without plagiarizing.
- For my students to learn how to find specific information in a nonfiction book.

- For my students to learn how to use nonfiction features such as subtitles and diagrams.
- For my students to write paragraphs about the key ideas or main ideas.
- For my students to present information in an interesting way.

As I approached this project with my third graders, I realized the only way to go about teaching them these skills was to model, model, and model as each new step was approached.

I showed my students an example of an Investigations project from a second grade class, and they were very impressed. I let them know that I would guide them through the steps involved, but they would need to use their creativity to put it all together.

The Investigations project had to include a title, informative written text on the four key ideas that was written in their own words, a diagram, and a border.

Another third-grade teacher (Shannon Hanson) and I developed a note-taking sheet that included four key topics, or main ideas. I modeled with a nonfiction book how I would go about finding information on one of the key ideas. This involved teaching them what to look for in the table of contents and how to use an index.

TOPIC: *Anaconda*   Scott

Details

Physical Characteristics
Weight
Height   *An Anaconda lives three to four years.*
Color   *The Eunectes murinus is Green and*
Life Span *E. murinus is Yellow.*

Details grassland desert polar ice forest ocean
country

Habitat

*The green Anaconda lives in the
Amazon and Orinoco rivers in the
tropics of south America. The yellow
Anaconda will go so far it will be by
Argentina.*

FIGURE 20.13 A sample note-taking sheet.

Then I modeled taking notes from the text and writing them on my sheet. This was one of the biggest lessons because I wanted them to learn how to write the factual information in their own words, avoiding plagiarism. After I had modeled this, I had them practice in groups before they tried it on their own. I gave them one of three different nonfiction animal books. They had to use the table of contents and index to figure out where to look for information on what that animal ate. This piece of the assignment was very helpful because they discovered some not so obvious table of contents titles to look under for information. They had to find and write down information about what that animal ate in their own words. When they were finished, I put them into the three animal groups and had them share what they had written. This was very powerful because what they discovered was they all had the same information, within each animal group, but they had written the sentences in their own words.

At this point I felt they were ready to begin using the books and taking notes on the animal they had chosen.

The next lessons taught how to take the notes and put them into a paragraph form with a lead-in or topic sentence. I showed examples of paragraphs that were nonfiction and how details are added without harming the integrity of the factual information. I wrote a paragraph for them about crocodiles from the notes I had taken earlier in this project. They wrote each paragraph on a note card, paying attention to the conventions of their writing.

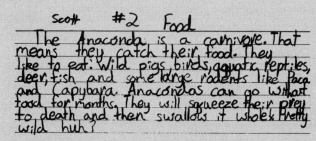

FIGURE 20.14 A sample of a paragraph card.

During this point in the investigations, I was teaching diagrams through my whole class shared reading as well as selecting nonfiction texts with diagrams for my guided reading groups. When it came time to teach diagrams for the investigations, they all had a solid idea of what they were. I gave them a square piece of paper to sketch their idea for their diagrams.

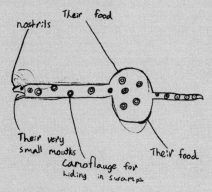

FIGURE 20.15 A planning sketch of a diagram.

The next two steps were the final touches. I modeled subtitles with some books and posters. We looked at how they made them stand out. We also talked about borders and how they made a final piece look finished. We discussed that this border would need to be different from some of the more decorative borders we had done with different art and writing activities. This border needed to have something to do with the animal they had chosen.

Through this process the students learned how to do research and a way of presenting it to many people. I believe these are skills that will serve them well throughout their school career!

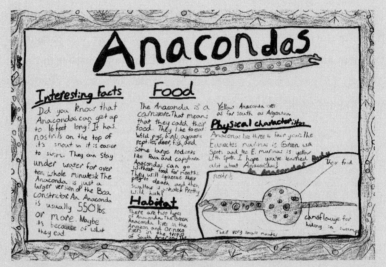

FIGURE 20.16

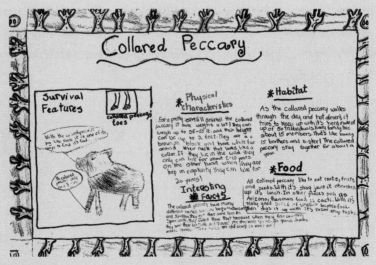

FIGURE 20.17
The third-grade Investigations.

Investigations

Diane Gast, Fourth-Grade Teacher, Bend, Oregon

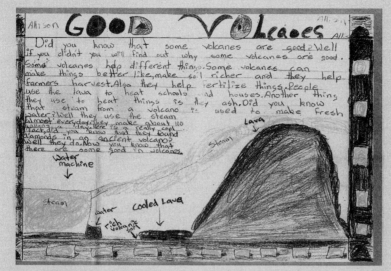

FIGURE 20.18

When I first tried Investigations, it was in conjunction with a science unit on earthquakes and volcanoes. My students are highly interested in this topic because in Bend we actually have an extinct volcano in the middle of town! Many students have lava flows in their backyards, and the Cascade Mountain Range is fifteen minutes from town.

To begin the science unit I asked the students what they knew or thought they knew about volcanoes and earthquakes. From this list I could determine which subtopics have been learned and which areas we need to work on further. I also asked students to write about what they would like to learn. With the experience base these students have, they generated quite an extensive list of subtopics for study.

After going through the two lists, I gleaned more than thirty subtopics of interest. I went to the library and checked out nonfiction books and found articles in different encyclopedias. Some students researched on the internet. We had a huge pile of information. It was more than a class could get through in a reasonable amount of time. I asked them if they would like to each take a subtopic, research it, and then present their information to the class. Each of us would be learners as well as teachers!

Since this was the first time my students had done an Investigation, I provided quite a bit of structure. I located sections of each book or article that contained information for a given subtopic and then gave each student a book or an article. We reviewed using the index and table of contents to locate information and discussed how to select passages. When doing an Investigation, we only need to read certain parts of the book. We reviewed how to use subtitles and boldface words. We scanned our text for diagrams, pictures, captions, tables, and graphs. Many students already had an idea of what they wanted in their final project by just looking at these. We talked about what a final project would look like and I shared several examples of work that students in another school had done. Each project had to include: a title, original written text, a diagram with labels and title, and a border.

Before getting into text, I modeled how I would read a piece of nonfiction. In nonfiction I told them I always read slower and make frequent stops to think about what it is I just read. Sometimes I even take notes. I brought in a nonfiction book I was using to facilitate a study group and showed them the highlighting and note taking I had done in the book. I also brought in some notes I had taken the past summer for a class. This, I explained to them, is how an adult reads and takes notes. We also addressed plagiarism and how to avoid it.

Students began reading their nonfiction selections. As they read they stopped frequently, thought about what it was that they were reading, and then summarized. We were trying to find at least five or six interesting facts. With these facts, our next step was to write a paragraph. Students helped each other with revision and editing. Once students were happy with their text, they began the process of making a diagram. The diagram needed to support the written text. Some students chose to ask a peer to look over the work done so far, and ask questions. These questions gave the writers ideas of where their text might be weak, and this also gave the writers ideas for diagrams that might explain, in picture form, some information. The final step in the rough draft process was that of designing a border for the project.

The final project was done on a piece of 11 × 17 paper. Students did a thumbnail sketch of where they wanted to place the text and diagram. They began by drawing the border around the perimeter of the paper. The text, diagram, and border were copied onto the project paper. The next step was to add color that drew the eye. We used what we had learned in art about contrasting color and positive and negative space. The final project was then mounted on colored construction paper and laminated. Students shared their final projects with the class.

My students really enjoyed doing this project. In the future, I will give them large sticky notes to take notes on, because then students can manipulate the order of ideas and facts. They would get really frustrated with the revision process because sometimes their paragraphs would sound choppy. Sticky notes give students more flexibility to move ideas into an order that flows and allows them to work out transitions. I really liked how writers took the questions other classmates would ask them during the revision process and use that to help make the writing and diagram more exact. I am looking forward to our next Investigation.

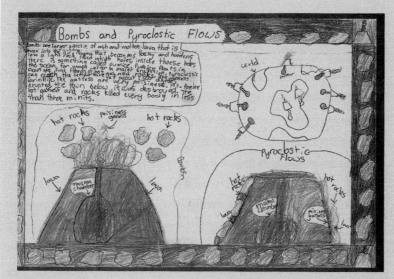

FIGURE 20.19 A fourth-grade volcano investigation.

Investigations Alphabet Books

Brenda Meenach, Fourth and Fifth Grade, Spokane, Washington

I used the fourth- and fifth-grade social studies curriculum and guided the students' review of the content through Investigations alphabet books.

I've seen real growth in kids' ability to find information using a variety of resources. They had to become proficient in using a table of contents and index and had to learn to skim and scan for the authentic purpose of reviewing content from the curriculum we have covered.

I have integrated this review and associated research strategies into guided reading. I also set aside specific times each day throughout the year for students to work on this project.

The kids love it so much, they even work on it during rainy day recesses.

I did face a few logistical challenges. I wanted this to also serve as handwriting practice so lines on the paper were a must. Last year I used unlined paper and they didn't look as nice. I tried the old marble composition books but they were too small. I have settled on spiral notebooks.

The half-inch border around each two-page layout takes several attempts for students to measure. This makes me feel like I'm teaching a life skill of measuring and I also hit it as a math target.

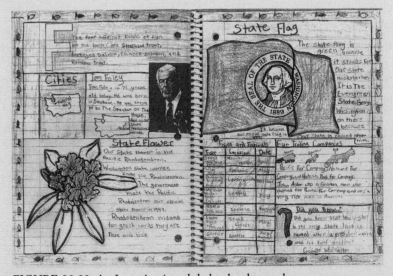

FIGURE 20.20 An Investigation alphabet book sample.

Raina Bohanek, a teacher in Spokane, Washington, developed the following innovation for Investigations. Here is a sample of one of her students' investigation.

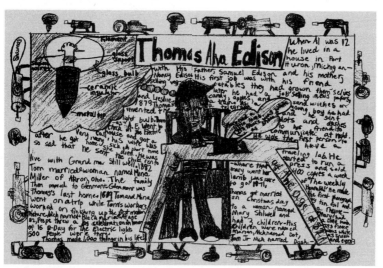

FIGURE 20.21 Here is an example of a hero investigation.

Hero Investigation Requirements

Name _____ Due Date _____

An investigation is an inquiry into a topic that is less in-depth than a full research paper, yet provides substantial details about a topic. When someone is finished reading and looking at your investigation, they should have a good understanding of your hero.

This investigation **must include** the following:
- Why this person is considered a hero. (Be specific, use examples)
- What accomplishments this person is known for
- Information on the person's early life and how that led them to become a hero
- Information on their adult life
- Why this person is your hero

You **may also include** some of these categories:
- Information about your hero's family
- Quotes from your hero and why they are significant
- Other information you find interesting

Requirements for the Design of the Investigation

_____ 1. A border that is an inch wide or the width of a ruler. The border must in some way tie in with the topic of your hero.

_____ 2. A title that describes your hero and is placed to grab the audience's attention.

_____ 3. A picture of your hero that you have imported from the computer.

_____ 4. Written information about your hero (see categories above). The information cannot be copied from books. It must be written in your own words and done on the computer. The subtopics you write about need to have headings so the reader knows what information is contained there.

_____ 5. All white space must be colored, but words still easy to read.

_____ 6. A bibliography must be attached to the back of the probe.

_____ 7. Your first and last name must be included in the lower right-hand corner of the border.

Bibliography

Allen, Janet. 2000. *Yellow Brick Roads: Shared and Guided Paths to Independent Reading 4–12.* Portland, ME: Stenhouse Publishers.

Allington, R. 2001. *What Really Matters for Struggling Students: Designing Research-Based Programs.* New York: Longman.

Anderson, R. et al. 1992. *Becoming a Nation of Readers.* Urbana, IL: Center for the Study of Readers.

Armstrong, J.O., M. Wise, C. Janisch, and L.A. Meyer. 1991. "Reading and Questioning in Content Area Lessons." *Journal of Reading Behavior* 23 No 1.

Atwell, N. ed. 1990. *Coming to Know: Writing to Learn in the Intermediate Grades.* Portsmouth, NH: Heinemann.

Bamford, Rosemary A., and Janice V. Kristo, eds. 1998. *Making Facts Come Alive: Choosing Quality Nonfiction Literature K–12.* Norwood, MA: Christopher Gordon.

Bamford, Rosemary A., and Janice V. Kristo, eds. 2000. *Checking Out Nonfiction K–8: Good Choices for Best Learning.* Norwood, MA: Christopher Gordon.

Batzle, Janine. 2001. Presentation for the Beaverton School District.

Block, Cathy Collins, and Michael Pressley, ed. 2002. *Comprehension Instruction: Research-Based Best Practices.* New York: The Guilford Press.

Buehl, Doug. 2001. *Classroom Strategies for Interactive Learning.* Newark, DE: International Reading Association.

Bridges, L. 1997. *Writing as a Way of Knowing.* Portland, ME: Stenhouse Publishers.

Bruner, J. 1978. "The Role of Dialogue in Language Acquisition." *In The Child's Conception of Language*, edited by A. Sinclair, R. Jarvella, and W. Levelt. New York: Springer-Verlag.

Calkins, Lucy. 2000. *The Art of Teaching Reading.* New York: Addison Wesley.

Camp, Deanne. 2000. "It Takes Two: Teaching with Twin Texts of Fact and Fiction." *The Reading Teacher* (February).

Cerullo, Mary M. 1997. *Reading the Environment: Children's Literature in the Science Classroom.* Portsmouth, NH: Heinemann.

Clay, M. 1991. *Becoming Literate: The Construction of Inner Control.* Portsmouth, NH: Heinemann.

Creenaune, T., and L. Rowles. 1996. *What's Your Purpose? Reading Strategies for Nonfiction Texts.* Sydney, Australia: Primary English Teachers Association.

Cruz, Payne C. 2000. *Guided Reading: Making It Work.* Jefferson County, MO: Scholastic Professional Books.

Cumming, J. 2000. *Language, Power and Pedagogy: Bilingual Children in the Crossfire.* Clevedon, UK: Multilingual Matters.

Cunningham, P., D. Hall, and C. Sigmon. 1999. *The Teacher's Guide to the Four Blocks.* Greensboro, NC: Carson-Dellosa.

Department of Education, Western Australia. 1995. *First Steps.* Portsmouth, NH: Heinemann.

Derewianka, B. 1990. *Exploring How Texts Work.* Sydney, Australia: Primary English Teaching Association.

Donovan, C., and L. Smolkin. 2002. "Considering Genre, Content, and Visual Features in the Selection of Trade Books for Science Instruction." *The Reading Teacher* 55 no 6. (March).

Donovan, Carol A., and Laura B. Smolkin. 2001. "Genre and Other Factors Influencing Teachers' Book Selection for Science Instruction." *Reading Research Quarterly* 36 (4): 412–440.

Dreher, Mariam Jean. 2002. "Children Searching and Using Informational Text." In *Comprehension Instruction: Research-Based Best Practices*, edited by Cathy Collins Block and Michael Pressley, 289–304. New York: The Guilford Press.

Duke, Nell K. 2000. "3–6 Minutes per Day: The Scarcity of Informational Texts in First Grade." *Reading Research Quarterly* 35 (2): 202–224.

Duthie, C. 1994. "Nonfiction: A Genre Study for the Primary Classroom." *Language Arts* 71: 588–594.

Duthie, C. 1996. *True Stories: Nonfiction in the Primary Classroom.* York, ME: Stenhouse.

Fisher, Andrea. 2001. "Implementing Graphic Organizer Notebooks: The Art and Science of Teaching Content." *The Reading Teacher* (October).

Fletcher, Ralph, and Joann Portalupi. 2001. *Nonfiction Craft Lessons: Teaching Informational Writing K–8.* York, ME: Stenhouse.

Forte, I., and S. Schurr. 1996. *Graphic Organizers and Planning Outlines for Authentic Instruction and Assessment.* Nashville, TN: Incentive Publications.

Fountas, Irene C., and Gay Su Pinnell. 1996. *Guided Reading: Good First Teaching for All Children.* Portsmouth, NH: Heinemann.

Fountas, Irene C., and Gay Su Pinnell. 2001. *Guided Readers and Writers Grades 3–6: Teaching Comprehension, Genre, and Content Literacy.* Portsmouth, NH: Heinemann.

Freedman, A., and P. Medway, eds. 1994. *Genre and the New Rhetoric.* Bristol, PA: Taylor and Francis.

Fry, E., J. Kress, and D. Fountoukidis. 2000. *The Reading Teacher's Book of Lists.* Paramus, NJ: Prentice Hall.

Gibbons, Pauline. 2002. *Scaffolding Language Scaffolding Learning: Teaching Second Language Learners in the Mainstream Classroom.* Portsmouth, NH: Heinemann.

Graves, Michael, and Bonnie Graves. 1994. *Scaffolding Reading Experiences: Designs for Student Success.* Norwood, MA: Christopher Gordon.

Green, P. 1992. *A Matter of Fact: Using Factual Texts in the Classroom.* Winnipeg: Peguis.

Guillaume, Andrea. 1998. "Learning with Text in the Primary Grades." *Reading Teacher* 51 (March): 476–486.

Harvey, Stephanie. 1998. *Nonfiction Matters: Reading, Writing and Research in Grades 3–8.* York, ME: Stenhouse Publishers.

Harvey, Stephanie, and Anne Goudvis. 2000. *Strategies That Work.* York, ME: Stenhouse Publishers.

Hoff, David. 2002. "US Students Rank Among World's Best and Worst Readers." *Education Week* (January).

Hoyt, L. 1992. "Many Ways of Knowing." *The Reading Teacher* 45 (April): 580–584.

Hoyt, Linda. 1999. *Revisit, Reflect, Retell: Strategies for Improving Reading Comprehension.* Portsmouth, NH: Heinemann.

Hoyt, Linda. 2000. *Snapshots: Literacy Minilessons Up Close.* Portsmouth, NH: Heinemann.

Hyerle, D. 1996. *Visual Tools for Constructing Knowledge.* Alexandria, VA: Association for Supervision and Curriculum Development.

Jobe, Ron, and Mary Dayton-Sakari. 2002. *Info-Kids: How to Use Non-fiction to Turn Reluctant Readers into Enthusiastic Learners.* York, ME: Stenhouse.

Keene, E.O., and S. Zimmerman. 1997. *Mosaic of Thought: Teaching Comprehension in a Reader's Workshop.* Portsmouth, NH: Heinemann.

Krashen, S. 1993. *The Power of Reading: Insights from Research.* Englewood, CO: Libraries Unlimited.

Mann, Charles. 2002. "1491." *Atlantic Monthly* (March): 41–53.

Marland, M. 1977. *Language Across the Curriculum.* London: Heinemann.

McCarrier, A., G. Pinnell, and I. Fountas. 2000. *Interactive Writing: How Language and Literacy Come Together, K–2.* Portsmouth, NH: Heinemann.

Meek, M. 1996. *Information and Book Learning.* Stroud, UK: Thimble Press.

Mohan, B. 2001. "The Second Language as Medium of Learning." In *English as a Second Language in the Mainstream: Teaching, Learning, and Identity*, edited by B. Mohan, C. Leung, and C. Davison. London: Longman.

Moline, Steven. 1995. *I See What You Mean: Children at Work with Visual Information.* Melbourne, Australia: Longman.

Mooney, Margaret E. 1990. *Reading to, with, and by Children.* Katonah, NY: Richard C. Owen Publishers, Inc.

Mooney, Margaret. 1995. *Exploring New Horizons with Guided Reading.* Worthington, OH: SRA Macmillan/McGraw-Hill.

Mooney, Margaret E. 2001. *Text Forms and Features: A Resource for Intentional Teaching.* Katonah, New York: Richard C. Owen Publishers, Inc.

National Reading Panel Report. 2001. National Institute for Child Health and Development.

Ogle, Donna, and Camille L.Z. Blachowicz. 2002. "Beyond Literature Circles, Helping Students Comprehend Informational Texts." In *Comprehension Instruction: Research-Based Best Practices*, edited by Cathy Collins Block and Michael Pressley, 259–274. New York: The Guilford Press.

Opitz, Michael, and Timothy Raskinski. 1998. *Good-Bye Round Robin: 25 Effective Oral Reading Strategies.* Portsmouth, NH: Heinemann.

Parkes, Brenda. 2000. *Read It Again: Revisiting Shared Reading.* York, ME: Stenhouse Publishers.

Peeck, J. 1987. "The Role of Illustrations in Processing and Remembering Illustrated Text." In *The Psychology of Illustration* 1. New York: Springer-Verlag.

Portalupi, Joann, and Ralph Fletcher. 2001. *Nonfiction Craft Lessons: Teaching Informational Writing K–8*. Portland, ME: Stenhouse.

Pressley, Michael. 2000. "What Should Comprehension Instruction Be the Instruction Of?" In *Handbook of Reading Research*, edited by M.L. Kamil, P.B. Mosenthal, P.D. Pearson, and R. Barr. Mahwah, NJ: Erlbaum.

Rice, Diana. 2002. "Using Trade Books in Teaching Elementary Science: Facts and Fallacies." *The Reading Teacher* 55 (March): 552–566.

Routman, R. 2000. *Conversations*. Portsmouth, NH: Heinemann.

Samway, Katharine Davies, and Gail Whang. 1996. *Literature Study Circles in a Multicultural Classroom*. York, ME: Stenhouse.

Schwartz, S., A. Klein, and R. Shook. 2001. *Interactive Writing and Interactive Editing: Making Connections Between Writing and Reading*. Carlsbad, CA: Dominie.

Secretary's Commission on Achieving Necessary Skills. 1992. *What Work Requires of Schools: A SCANS Report for America 2000*. Washington DC: U.S. Department of Labor.

Stead, T. 2001. *Is That a Fact?: Teaching Nonfiction Writing K–3*. York, ME: Stenhouse Publishers.

Taberski, Sharon. 2000. *On Solid Ground: Strategies for Teaching Reading K–3*. Portsmouth, NH: Heinemann.

Taylor, B., P.D. Pearson, K. Clar, and S. Walpole. 1999. *Beating the Odds in Teaching Children to Read, Lessons from Effective Schools and Exemplary Teachers*. Michigan: CIERA.

Walpole, S. 1999. "Changing Texts, Changing Thinking: Changing Demands of New Science Textbooks." *The Reading Teacher* 52: 357–370.

Wormeli, R. 2001. "Writing in the Content Areas." In *Meet Me in the Middle*. York, ME: Stenhouse Publishers.

Yatvin, Joanne. 2002. "Babes in the Woods: The Wanderings of the National Reading." *Phi Delta Kappa* (January): 364–369.

Yatvin, Joanne. 2002. "The Many Faces of Reading Research: Views from a National Reading Panel Member." Presentation at Portland State University.

Yopp, Ruth Helen, and Hallie Kay Yopp. 2000. "Sharing Informational Text with Young Children." *The Reading Teacher* (February).